Legal Guide
for
Police
and
Citizens

Attention Authors

'We Convert Fighters into Writers.' That's the motto of Manas Publications since more than four decades. Our message to the world is that India can win the battle not only by the bullet but also by the pen. There is no dearth of intellectuals in our country, but their knowledge is confined to them only. No sincere effort has been made by any other publisher to channelise their knowledge in national interest. That is why the talent of a large number of intellectuals remains latent. An author transforms his knowledge into a manuscript, and it is our job to spread his/her knowledge by converting it into a beautiful book. For over four decades, Manas has been motivating the intellectuals by publishing their manuscripts and would like to publish your manuscript too. If you or your colleagues have any manuscript ready for publication or are working on it, kindly contact us with detailed synopsis and list of contents. We will transform your work into a valuable publication. If you wish, we can also suggest you the suitable subjects for writing the books related to your area of expertise. Manas is known for its publishing quality and commitments. We take utmost care in production and give wide publicity to the book as well as its author through our national and international distribution network.

Legal Guide
for
Police
and
Citizens

SP Kar, IPS (Retd)

(Former IGP - Assam)

Manas Publications

(We Convert Fighters into Writers)

New Delhi-110002 (India)

MANAS PUBLICATIONS

(Publishers for IAS, IPS, IFS, IRS, Defence, Press, Judges etc)

4402/5-A, Ansari Road (Opp HDFC Bank)
Darya Ganj, New Delhi-110 002 (India)
Off.: 23260783, 23265523, Fax: 011-23272766
E-mail: manaspublications@gmail.com
manaspublications@yahoo.com

ISBN:978-81-7049-459-1

Rs 495/-

Designed at: **Manas Publications**

Printed in India at
Rajdhani Printers, Delhi
and published by Mrs Suman Lata for
Manas Publications, 4402/5-A,
Ansari Road (Opp HDFC Bank),
Darya Ganj, New Delhi-110 002 (INDIA)

Contents

Introduction

In the present day situation, the police have multifarious functions to perform. Among other things, their task is to prevent and detect crimes, provide security to the citizens, maintain law and order, fight insurgency and extend a helping hand to other departments of the government. Even non-governmental organisations very often seek the help of the police in many fields. All this keeps the police extremely busy, particularly because the manpower available with them is inadequate. These causes cumulatively make it very difficult for the individual police officer to keep abreast of developments in the field of law from which they draw sustenance.

During my tenure of office in different capacities, I drew the experience that an average police officer suffered from a lack of adequate information on a wide canvas of legal matters. Non-availability of a compendium of such information adds to this problem.

The present compilation is a response to the above. I have used herein information available in the public domain, though the views given are entirely my own. Sources of information inserted in the book have been indicated at the appropriate places. For further elaboration, reference may be made to me over telephone or e-mail or by post.

SP Kar, IPS (Retd)

Chapter - I

Basic Laws for the Police

The police are an arm of the law. Law gets expression in the acts of the police. They are the most visible symbol of the State whose prime duty is to uphold the rule of law.[1] People, by seeing how fairly and efficiently the police function in a particular State or a given area, can have a perception of the nature of governance that the citizens are having from their government.[i]

Any visible or even invisible act of corruption indulged in by a policeman is a manifestation of the regime - to which he belongs - being corrupt. When a policeman on a public road raises one of his hands towards the cabin of a truck driver, the sight leaves no one in doubt about the fact that he was extorting money from the latter. This brings the government into disrepute and governance to an utter failure. The efficiency of the regime in providing good governance gets reflected in the efficiency of the police force in their essential functions. The government's care for the well-being of the citizens gets mirrored on the care shown by policemen in helping out the distressed. There are innumerable instances of distressed individuals, male or female, seeking succor from the police even when the cause of distress has nothing to do with police functions. This is because the people, being ignorant or oblivious of the precise role of the police, take it as a physical arm of the state. However, the police have basically to remain an agency of the state for maintenance of law and order and initiation of the process of criminal justice. All this necessitates the exercise of legal power by the police as a legal entity. Law therefore must recognize the police as a legal entity and specifically lay down its functions.

---

1 Rule of law is a system where it is the law–and not the whims and caprices of the men in power – that prevails. It is the essence of a democratic system.

The Police Act, 1861

The institution of police had existed in India, in some form or the other, throughout the ancient and middle ages of history. However, as the regimes of kings and sultans in those times were autocratic and functioned on the individual wishes and whims of the rulers, their police were no better. There existed hardly any written law, except probably some conventions, to regulate the conduct and functions of the police of the yesteryears.[2] It was the British who, for the first time, codified a law called the Police Act in the year 1861 to give a legal foundation for police functions. It goes to the credit of the great English law-makers of the mid-19th century India that the Police Act 1861, framed nearly one and a half centuries back from now, still remains the foundation of the police law in the country. The later legislations on the police in free India evolved from this piece of law.

The police have been made a State subject under the Seventh Schedule of the Constitution of India. This means the Government of a State has all the powers and responsibility to manage, supervise and control the police force in all functions, and provide the necessary funds and wherewithal for its working.

The following were the special features of the Police Act 1861 passed originally by the British government as an all-India Act to be applicable all over British India.[3] The Act continued to be uniformly in force in all states and union territories even after Independence in 1947 and the coming into force of the Constitution of India in 1950.

1. The IGP[4] will administer the police in the State subject to the direct control of the State Government. .
2. The District SP will similarly administer the police in his District subject to the general control of the District Magistrate.
3. The SP in the District or an officer of equivalent rank in an armed police battalion and other police organisations will be the

---

2 The concept of written laws was virtually unknown in India before the arrival of the British in the country.

3 The term 'British India' covered all the provinces in India directly under the control of the British Government and it excluded the 560-odd princely states, which were ruled by Indian princes under the paramountcy – the paramount power – of the British crown.

4 The later day Directors General of Police (since 1979) drew their legal powers as the IGP in charge of the State Police.

disciplinary authority for police personnel up to and inclusive of the rank of Sub-Inspector.

4. In respect of Inspectors, the IGP will be the disciplinary authority.
5. The State Government shall be the disciplinary authority for all gazetted officers.

   [This follows the provision of Article 311 of the Constitution where the basic theme is that the appointing authority shall also be the disciplinary authority.]
6. Subordinate police officers shall have an *appointment certificate* by virtue of which they will be deemed to have been vested with all police powers.
7. The Police Manuals prepared under the authority of and approved by the State Government shall have the force of law.
8. Special Police Officers (SPOs) may be appointed by the District Magistrate concerned from among local people to control riots, etc. Such SPOs will have police powers.[5]
9. Police officers shall obey and execute all lawful orders. The emphasis is on the lawfulness of the order. Even if 'a higher authority' issues an unlawful order, it will not be lawful to execute it. The responsibility remains with the officer concerned. In the international field also, the plea that an unlawful action was taken by a functionary of the state on orders of his superiors has been emphatically rejected.[6]
10. Among the other duties of the police laid down in the 1861 Act, the following were notable:
    (a) Collection and communication of intelligence (that is advance information).
    (b) Prevention and detection of crimes.
    (c) Prevention of all kinds of public nuisance.

---

5 This provision is being increasingly used in Assam and Manipur for creating additional manpower (as an auxiliary to the available police forces) to combat insurgency-related crimes.

6 The Nuremberg trial in 1945 of Nazi war criminals had conclusively established the universal legal norm that the perpetrator of an outrage on the life and rights of citizens shall bear full responsibility for his actions regardless of whatever orders he had received from his superiors. The deliberations of the post-Emergency Shah Commission also upheld the above principle against the plea of superior's verbal orders for wrong doings.

The National Police Commision, 1977

No comprehensive review of the working of the police in India (or of the 1861 Police Act) was done in the immediate post-Independence years though, in the meantime, especially after the end of World War II, there had occurred tremendous changes in the political, social and economic situation in the country. The Constitution that came into force on January 26, 1950 conferred on citizens a number of fundamental rights[7] that were unthought of during the British rule. The police in India, however, continued to function in its old colonial pattern, regardless of the change – the transformation of India from a subject nation to a nation of free citizens - that had since occurred. In this vacuum, the state of Emergency imposed by the then Prime Minister Indira Gandhi on June 26, 1975 resulted in a massive misuse of the existing police machinery in the country and therefore added a new question-mark about the precise role of the police in the life of citizens. Considering these developments, the Government of India, then led by a Janata Party-led coalition, appointed on 15th November, 1977 a National Police Commission, with Dharam Vira, ICS, a former Governor of West Bengal, as Chairman, to make a "fresh examination of the role and performance of the police both as a law-enforcing agency and as an institution to protect the rights of the citizens enshrined in the Constitution."[8] The terms of reference for the Commission required it, among other things, to redefine the role, duties, powers and responsibilities of the police with special reference to the prevention and control of crime and maintenance of public order.

The Commission examined in depth all the related issues and submitted to the Government its report in eight parts over a period of three and a half years. It recommended a number of radical changes

7 The Fundamental Rights were designed on the line of the Universal Declaration of Human Rights, 1948.

8 It is remarkable that the appointment of the Commission came in the wake of the 'Internal Emergency' (1975-77) during which there had been obnoxious abuse of police powers all over India. The police were used by the powers-that-be as a tool to curb the fundamental rights (right to life and liberty among other things) of citizens during the period. This black period in the history of India witnessed innumerable cases of arbitrary detentions, harassment, custodial torture and deaths for which the police were primarily responsible.

in the country's policing system to make the institution of police a protector of the rights of citizens as well as accountable to law. For all this, the police had to be functionally independent and not subject to extra-legal political and bureaucratic control. However, the Government of India did not initiate any step to implement the recommendations of the Commission even as years passed by.

PIL for police reforms

Flabbergasted with the total indifference of the Central and State Governments to the need for bringing about reforms in the colonial set-up and functioning of the police, some public-spirited citizens, led by Prakash Singh,[9] filed under Article 32 of the Constitution a Writ Petition[10] before the Supreme Court of India in 1996 praying for the issue of directions to the Government of India to frame a new Police Act on the lines of the model Act drafted by the National Police Commission to make the police primarily accountable to the law of the land and the people.

The Supreme Court Bench presided over by the then Chief Justice of India, Justice YK Sabharwal, considered in depth the plea made in the Writ Petition and issued on September 22nd, 2006 the following directions to the Government of India, the State Governments and the Union Territory Administrations:

1. The police being a State subject under the Constitution, the State Governments should enact their own State Police Acts on the recommended lines. The legislation is to be based on and include the recommendations of the National Police Commission and the other bodies that deliberated on the subject of police reforms in recent times, like the National Human Rights Commission, the Law Commission of India, the Rebeiro Committee, the Malimath Committee and the Soli Sorabjee Committee. The underlying aim behind these recommendations is the introduction of positive accountability of the police to rule of law. [In this connection, the NN Vohra Committee had earlier indicated that there was in India a strong police-politics-mafia nexus, which was a great deal responsible for failed governance in the country.]

---

9 A retired IPS officer, Prakash Singh is a former Director General of Police of Assam, UP and the Border Security Force.

10 WP (Civil) No. 310 of 1996 (Prakash and Others *vs* Union of India and Others) (SC).

2. Pending the passing of an appropriate law to govern the functioning of the police, the State Governments will take the following actions:

(a) A State Security Commission will be constituted for laying down broad policy guidelines for the functioning of the State Police. Headed by the State Chief Minister or the Home Minister, the Commission will be independent of 'governmental control' to see that the police always act according to the laws of the land and the Constitution. The State DGP will be the ex-officio secretary of this watchdog body. The recommendations of the body will be binding on the Government.

(b) The Director General of Police of the State is to be chosen from among officers empanelled for the rank by the Union Public Service Commission on the basis of seniority and service record. Once selected, he shall have a minimum tenure of two years irrespective of his date of superannuation. However, the Security Commission may recommend his removal in certain exigencies.

(c) Officers in field duties like an IGP (Zone), a DIG (Range), an SP of a District or an Officer-in-Charge of a Police Station will have a similar two-year tenure at the minimum, unless removed or transferred in certain given situations.

(d) To facilitate better and speedier investigation of criminal cases, the investigation branch of the police is to be separated from the law and order branch.

(e) A Police Establishment Board is to be set up in each State to decide on all transfers, postings, promotions and other service-related matters in respect of officers of and below the rank of Deputy Superintendent of Police (Dy SP). The Board will be a departmental body comprising the DGP and four other senior officers of the department.

(f) There shall be a Police Complaints Authority in every District, headed by a retired District Judge, to look into complaints against officers of and below to the rank of Dy SP. Similarly, at the State level, a Police Complaint Authority has to be constituted with a retired High Court/ Supreme Court Judge as chairman. The recommendations of these Authorities will be binding on the government or the departmental authorities concerned.

(g) There is to be a National Security Commission at the Centre in respect of Central Police Organisations like the CRPF, BSF, etc. Its line of work will be similar to that of the State Security Commissions.

The Assam Police Act, 2007

Some of the States have already passed their own Police Acts following the above judgment of the Supreme Court. In Assam, for example, the newly enacted Assam Police Act, 2007, which replaced the 1861 Act, came into force on August 31, 2007. Apart from retaining the general tenor and features of the 1861 Act, the new Assam Police Act introduced some new concepts in policing, trying to keep pace with the developments that have taken place since 1861, especially since the promulgation of independent India's Constitution on January 26, 1950. The following are some of the notable features of the Assam Police Act, 2007.

1. The Act has a preamble, which expressly mentions the constitutional obligation of the State to provide an impartial, efficient and professionally organised Police Force for safeguarding the interests of the people based on the ideal of rule of law. The Act behoves the police to be service-oriented while performing their mandatory duties of prevention and detection of crimes. It recognises the responsibility of the police in meeting the newly emerging challenges to the security of the State.[ii] Simultaneously, they have to be mindful of the fundamental rights of the citizens while performing their onerous duties.

   While impartiality - the essence of Article 14 of the Constitution - is a state of mind that needs culture in the broader social field, the efficiency of the police depends entirely on the quality of professional training that is imparted. The imbibing in the minds of policemen of a sense of commitment for the safety, security and welfare of the society need be a part of this training. Unfortunately, this aspect is totally neglected in our country. Lack of investment in police training, including the training of trainers,[11] has left us with extreme incompetence on the part of the police officers

11 The reality is that personnel rejected for public duties in the field for reasons of incompetence, corrupt practices or indiscipline are often inducted in police training institutions as instructors. It is done as a measure of punishment to these recalcitrant officers. This policy, a contradiction in itself, need be corrected if the objectives of the Act are to be achieved.

mandated to handle matters relating to people's life and property and delivery of justice. Even though there have been tremendous developments in the world in the field of technologies and forensic science which could be made use of fruitfully in investigation and intelligence-gathering, police officers at the cutting edge, like sub-inspectors and inspectors, are not given exposure to the new techniques available. These officers, therefore, continue to follow the archaic methods – modern at that time - initiated by the British in India one and a half centuries back.

2. The Act provides for a State Security Commission, a Police Establishment Board and a Police Accountability Commission (in place of a Police Complaints Authority) as recommended by the National Police Commission and directed by the Supreme Court.

   As per reports, these bodies have already been constituted and made functional in the State. However, the matter of their functional autonomy is a question of facts on the ground. It is hoped that with the passage of time, it would be possible to analyse whether these bodies made any significant difference in the working of the police in the State in any way.

3. The Act mandates the separation of the investigation wing of the police from its law and order wing. This point has been talked about for decades without any tangible action being taken. The intended measure, at the first instance, requires the enlargement of the Police Force by creation of a proportionate number of posts in all ranks at the police station level[12] and earmarking of officers of proven ability for investigation. As it is, though stricken by numerous problems of gigantic dimensions like escalating ethnic insurgencies, Jehadi terrorism and Bangladeshi influx, the sanctioned strength of the police stations in the State continues, as a rule, to remain stagnant for decades on end. The question here will be one of making a realistic assessment of the strength of personnel required to accomplish the tasks mandated for the police in the State keeping in view the increase in population, the rise in the crime rate and the other complexities that have arisen out of rapid urbanisation, industrialisation and globalisation during the last few decades. Sanction of the required posts, and recruitment

---

12 The Assam Police is, by any account, a top-heavy Force. It's perceivable that in the top echelon, many officers do not have enough work to do. On the other hand, at the police station level, officers are overburdened, so much so that investigation of cases takes the lowest priority. The quality of investigation, therefore, takes a beating.

and training of the personnel should follow in right earnest. This, however, cannot be a one-time process. Review in the same lines has to take place periodically, maybe after every ten years.

4. The Act lays down a comprehensive set of duties and responsibilities for the police. They include, among other things, the upholding of the law, human rights and dignity of individuals, maintenance of public order, internal security and communal harmony, protection of public property, prevention and detection of crimes, compulsory registration of FIRs,[iii] extension of all possible assistance to people during natural disasters and man-made conflicts and collection and collation of intelligence on matters relating to public peace and national security.

A very significant feature of the Act is that it imposes certain social responsibilities on the members of the police force. The police have been put under obligation to maintain courtesy and decorum (something that is rare in the colonial legacy inherited), to go forward to help women, children, senior citizens and others who need such help and to give succour to people facing harassment at public places.

The Act specifies some penalties for dereliction of duties by subordinate police officers and men. However, protection from frivolous accusation has been provided for.

Overall, the Assam Police Act 2007 has not altered, in any significant measure, the status of the police from what had existed during the British rule. In fact the subordination of the police to the executive continues as before. The intention of the National Police Commission and other bodies that had deliberated on the issue of police reforms was to make the police an independent and responsible organ of the state accountable only to law. This has not happened under the present Act.

The enactment of the Police Act is aimed at providing better policing to the people. This can be achieved only when the government can groom up better policemen who would understand the nuances of a people-friendly law and order system. Raising the educational qualification for the grassroots level policemen at the point of entry to the organisation is not the only answer to the question. The police personnel need be given a better life, free of unnecessary tension and frustration. A perpetually overworked policeman is not the correct person for people-friendly policing. He cannot be expected to present a pleasant personality, an attribute needed for the purpose.

To be suitable for the purpose, he also needs rest and leisure like any other normal person. More so because there is so much of expectation from him. He is under scrutiny by everybody, regardless of the difficult conditions of his work. Making adequate number of personnel available and a proper plan for their upkeepment are therefore required to meet these problems. Provision of reasonably comfortable accommodation for the men and their families and a pay scale appropriate for them in the current state of the economy is a *sine qua non* for a good police force. Thus, the implementation of the Act presupposes a lot of groundwork.

The Constitution of India

The Constitution of India adopted in 1950 is the fundamental law of the country. It is the law of laws. All previous laws in force since before the Independence as well as those enacted later must conform to the Constitution, otherwise they will become void.

Fundamental Rights guaranteed in Part III of the Constitution are central to all police functioning. These rights apply to all citizens; some of them apply even to non-citizens, like the right to life and liberty. However, so far as the police are concerned, the following aspects and provisions of the Constitution are very important:

Article 21 - Right to life and liberty

'No person shall be deprived of his life or personal liberty except according to procedure established by law.' Essentially, the basic duty of the police relates to this right. The very existence of the police is meant to ensure that the life and liberty of all persons in their jurisdiction are safe and secure from any unlawful ingress or attack. When the police fail in protecting this right, it is not only they but also the state that fails. Vibrant recent examples of the failure of the police in this regard were the anti-Sikh riots of 1984 in Delhi and anti-Muslim riots of 2002 in Gujarat when hundreds of innocent people lost their lives. When a custodial death or rape or assault takes place, it is the grossest violation of this right that takes place and the worst part of the irony is that such violence is inflicted by those who are mandated to be protectors of the victims.

The High Court concerned or the Supreme Court can award compensation under 'the Public Law' to the victim or his or her family for violation of the rights under this Article.

The Supreme Court has, from time to time, laid down some important principles under Article 21 in the following cases related to the police.

(i) The State of Tamil Nadu was ordered to pay a compensation of Rs 50,000/- to a lady who was illegally detained by the police. [Meera *vs* State of Tamil Nadu (1991) CrLJ 2395 (Mad)]

(ii) Imprisonment or incarceration of a person is unconstitutional after that person is declared insane. [Veena *vs* State of Bihar, AIR 1983 SC 339]

(iii) Custodial death is one of the worst crimes in a civilised society. The court hearing a writ petition on such a death may award compensation under the Public Law. [DK Basu *vs* State of West Bengal, AIR 1997 SC 610/SCC 416]

(iv) The right against custodial violence arises from Article 21. [Sheela Barse *vs* State of Punjab, AIR 1983 SC 378]

(v) Inordinate delay in bringing an accused to trial violates Article 21. [State of Rajasthan *vs* Sukhpal, AIR 1984 SC 207; State of Maharashtra *vs* Champalal, AIR 1981 SC 1675]

[Police officers keeping investigation of serious cases pending without sufficient justification should take note of this judgment.]

(vi) Cruel or torturous punishment is unconstitutional. [Inderjeet *vs* State of UP, AIR 1979 SC 1867]

(vii) In Sahali *vs* Commissioner of Police (AIR 1990 SC 513), some police officers had, at the behest of a landlord, beaten up lady tenant "K" and her minor son "N". The child succumbed to the injuries caused by the assault. The Court ordered the Delhi Administration to pay a certain amount of compensation to the aggrieved lady. This was in addition to the criminal prosecution that was to be launched against the guilty police officials. The compensation included –

(a) solatium for mental pain;

(b) solatium for distress and indignity;

(c) damages for loss of liberty;

(d) damages for death;

The Court directed the Delhi Administration to realize the amount from the officers responsible for the incident. The criminal prosecution to follow was to be for wrongful detention, assault and murder.

(viii) Child offenders are entitled to a speedy trial. [Sheela Barse *vs* Union of India, AIR 1986, SC 1773]

(ix) Right to life includes the right to health. [State of Punjab *vs* M.S.Chawla AIR 1997 SC 1225]

(x) In PV Kapoor *vs* Union of India [1992 Cr.L.J 140 DEL], the Delhi High Court awarded a compensation for the death of a person treated inhumanly by the police.

(xi) When a person violates with a malicious intent the constitutional and legal rights of another, the court can compensate the victim by awarding a suitable compensation. [Bhim Singh *vs* State of J & K 1986 CrLJ 192; Nilavati Behara *vs* State of Orissa (1993) 2 SCC 746]

(xii) Natural justice is implicit in Article 21. [Sunil Batra *vs* Delhi Administration AIR 1978 SC 1675]

(xiii) Solitary confinement violates Article 21. [Sunil Batra's case]

(xiv) Telephone tapping is a violation of privacy and therefore of Article 21.

(xv) In Kharak Singh *vs* State of UP (AIR 1963 SC 1295), the validity of police regulations that authorised surveillance by the police on History Sheeters was questioned. Surveillance by the police includes secret picketing of the home of the subject, domiciliary visits thereto at night and covert watch on his movements. It was contended that the said regulations violated the citizens' personal freedom granted by Article 19(1) and personal liberty enshrined in Article 21. The Supreme Court in a majority judgment held that the impugned regulation violated the right under Article 21 in so far as it authorized domiciliary visits but the rest of it was free from fault.

(xvi) In State of Maharashtra *vs* Madukar Narange Mandikar (1991 I SCC 57), the Supreme Court has held that even a woman of easy virtue is entitled to privacy and no one can invade her privacy as and when he likes.

(xvii) The Supreme Court, by pronouncement from time to time, has made the Right to life a repository of various other human rights like –

- the right to live with human dignity,

- the right to healthy environment,
- protection against hazardous industries,
- free education up to 14 years of age,[13]
- emergency medical aid,
- right to privacy,
- right to shelter,
- right not to be driven out of the state of domicile, (e.g., the case of Chakmas of Arunachal Pradesh)
- right to fair trial,
- right to speedy trial,

In the now famous BMW hit-and-run case, one Sanjeev Nanda, belonging to a rich and powerful family, was accused of mowing down six persons, including three policemen, with his BMW car in Delhi in January 1999. It was a sensational case, which the police commendably charge-sheeted within three months – and that too under section 304 IPC (culpable homicide not amounting to murder). But the law's delay was such that the final verdict in it came out at the court of sessions as late as in September 2008, thankfully, however, with conviction of the accused. The delay, which is usual with most of the criminal trials in the country, shook the confidence of the families of the victims in the efficacy of law. The verdict in the 1993 Mumbai Blast case (charge-sheeted in 1994) took a long fourteen years to be delivered by the TADA court concerned, which means that it may take another few years in the least before the appeals in them are disposed of by the Supreme Court.[14]

The Supreme Court has said that the impact of delay in the trial of criminal cases has a contrasting effect on the rich and the poor, conceding that it was far easier for the high and mighty person accused in a case to prolong the trial proceedings. A bench comprising Chief Justice KG Balakrishnan and Justice *vs* Sirpurkar said that a poor accused suffers the delay but the rich and influential enjoys the delay in a trial. The court agreed with

13 Article 21A has been added by a constitutional amendment in 2002 to recognize the right independently.

14 Appeals in the cases under the TADA (P) Act 1985 go directly to the Supreme Court.

counsel Prashant Bhushan that it was easy for a rich accused to delay the trial proceedings through various means – challenging every order of the trial court, influencing the witnesses and seeking adjournment on one ground or the other.[iv]

- right to free legal aid,
- right against sexual harassment at workplace,

[Vishaka *vs* State of Rajasthan, AIR 1997 SC 3011],

Sexual harassment includes gender-based advances, embarrassing jokes, showing of sex-oriented visuals, demand for sexual favour, etc. As per this judgment of the apex court, all governmental and non-governmental establishments in the country shall have a committee each to ensure a clean and free environment for the women working there.

(xviii) Non-production of a UTP[15] at the court at the end of the remand is a serious violation of the right to life.

It sometimes happens that a police officer arrests a person on suspicion under section 41 of the CrPC and forwards him to judicial custody forgetting all about the person's fate later. The arrestee thus spends any length of time in jail running into years without any redress. The following two episodes show how far things can go in this country:

54 years as an under trial prisoner?

"The Supreme Court on January 9, 2006 awarded an interim compensation of Rs 3 lakh to the septuagenarian Machang Lalung, who spent a total of 54 years in jail and a mental asylum in Assam as an undertrial. The court also ordered a high level enquiry by the State Government in to the case." [PTI]

In November 1950, Lalung, hailing from Mikir Chuburi village in Morigaon district of Assam, was arrested by the police under section 326 IPC on the charge of 'voluntarily causing grievous injuries' to a person. He was 23 years old then and when he came out without facing any trial in the court of law, he was 77.

The Gauhati High Court had earlier submitted a report to the Supreme Court following a directive from the latter to furnish an explanation as to why the case had been handled in such a manner that the man had to spend his youth in jail and left to rot in Tezpur mental

15 UTP – Under Trial Prisoner

asylum without a single hearing in any trial court. The apex court, taking cognizance of a letter submitted by an advocate and treating it as a PIL, has also sought a status report from the State Government. Meanwhile, the Chief Judicial Magistrate of Tezpur released Lalung from the mental asylum there following the intervention of the National Human Rights Commission and caused him to be handed over to his relations back home.

Enquiries revealed that Lalung, booked under section 326 IPC, was sent as an undertrial prisoner to Guwahati Jail in November 1950. In January 1951 he was declared to be a mental patient 'who was incapable of making his defence'. Following a court order in this line, the tribal villager was shifted to the LGB Regional Institute of Mental Health, Tezpur (LGB RIMH) in April 1951. It was further found that the records relating to the case in the court had been missing for a length of 22 years, comprising two 'time blocks' from 1951 to 1957 (both inclusive) and from 1979 to 1993 (both inclusive). However the available records indicate that the LGB RIMH authorities had, in two letters, issued on July 22, 1967 and August 10, 1967 to the Jail authorities and the State Law Department respectively, stated that Lalung was fit to stand trial. In 1994 the hospital authorities further informed the Kamrup District Magistrate that 'Lalung had fully recovered'. However, all this failed to evoke any response from the authorities concerned. No one knows what had happened to the police diary that would perhaps have shown if there was any evidence to prosecute the hapless man.[v]

This incident is a grim reminder to the magistracy that there could be injustice of such a formidable dimension that later there would be no remedy left for it if proper supervision and control is not maintained by the courts on the process of investigation and trial of cases before them. This is so vital for the justice system to work. Had the magistrates concerned over the years been vigilant enough to monitor the progress of the investigation of the case and also of the recovery process of the UTP at the mental hospital, Lalung's life would not have been rendered so meaningless at the age of 77 years. [The unfortunate man died within two years of release from jail.]

A case of 38 years without trial

In a similar story, one Jagjivan Ram, hailing from a village near Faizabad in UP, was arrested in 1968 for alleged murder by him of his neighbour's wife and he still awaits trial at Faizabad (in 2006). He was last produced at the court on Dec.7, 1968. Responding to a newspaper report, the Supreme Court issued notices to the Government of UP and the Allahabad High Court, seeking an explanation as to why Jagjivan Ram was detained so long and without trial. The story came to light when the Jail authorities concerned brought this to the notice of the Faizabad court in July 2005. Meanwhile, the police have reported to the court that the records of the case at the police station were untraceable and therefore they were unable to provide much information on it. A report from the Jail authorities showed that Jagjivan Ram was sent to Varanasi for treatment as per an executive order dated Dec.7, 1968, as 'he was mentally ill'. Even at the time of reporting of this episode in February 2006, the court was unable to grant bail to him because the nature of the charges against him was not clear.[vi]

Article 20

1. No person shall be convicted of any offence except for violation of law in force at the time of the commission of the act charged as an offence, nor be subjected to a penalty greater than that which might have been inflicted under the law in force at the time of the commission of the offence.
2. No person shall be prosecuted and punished for the same offence more than once.
3. No person accused of any offence shall be compelled to be a witness against himself.

This article is a safeguard against infliction of punishment by an *ex post facto* law, - that is, a law that takes a retrospective effect to cover an offence committed before the law was actually legislated.

Secondly, it also protects a person from being victimised for a second time for an offence for which he has already been prosecuted and tried. This is regardless of the outcome of the trial, whether it was conviction or acquittal. This provision is a protection against double jeopardy.

Thirdly, an accused person has the right to silence under Indian jurisprudence and therefore he cannot be coerced into making a statement that may be used as evidence against him in criminal proceedings. The accused should not be asked to make an averment *on oath*. Any statement or confession to be made by an accused has to be voluntary even in police interrogation. [Nandini Sathpathy *vs* PL Dani, 1978 25 SC 424]

So far as Article 20(2) is concerned, the apex court has made it clear in SA Vekataraman *vs* Union of India [AIR 1954 SC 375] that the holding of a departmental or other type of enquiry before or after criminal prosecution on the same subject matter does not amount to double jeopardy.

Article 14

The State shall not deny to any person equality before law.

This is an article of faith in our Constitution. The benefits from the principle laid down in it are available to all persons (and not confined to citizens alone). For the police who are mandated to be just and fair to all, this principle is of very high importance. As it is, the police have a reputation of being always pro-ruler and pro-rich and, therefore, this principle need be the working "mantra" for all ranks.

Equality before law entails reasonableness and absence of arbitrariness. A police officer, if he is to uphold the principles of Article 14 in his dealings with the public (which includes the maintenance of law and order, investigation of crime, etc.), he must be thoughtfully reasonable and shun all bias without a tinge of fear or favour.

Article 22

Under this article, it is the duty of the police to inform the arrestee (immediately after arrest) of the grounds of arrest and provide facility to him to consult a lawyer of his choice. It also lays down a time limit of 24 hours (excluding the time taken in journey) for the police to produce the arrested person before a magistrate.

The provisions of Section 50 and 57 CrPC have been made in consonance with this article.

Article 32 and 226

Any person, whose fundamental rights have been violated by any state action or an action of any of the agencies of the state, including local authorities, can move the Supreme Court (under Article 32) or the High Court concerned (under Article 226) for issue of a writ. A writ could be of the nature of *Habeas Corpus* or *Mandamus* or Prohibition or *Certiorari* or *Quo-warranto*, depending upon the relief sought by the petitioner. This is the last resort of a person, whether he is a government servant or a member of the public, to seek an immediate relief against any arbitrary action by the Union or State Government or any governmental agency.

Public Interest Litigation (PIL)

Rule of Law demands access of the poor and the weak to justice in equal measure with the rich and the powerful. However, in India, the poor face various social and economic handicaps to reach the portal of justice, partly because they are ignorant of the related processes and partly owing to huge expenses and time involved in litigations. To mitigate this problem, judicial activism of the recent years has emerged as a big help for the justice delivery system. Using the powers conferred on them by Article 32 and 226 of the Constitution, the higher judiciary (i.e. the Supreme Court and the High Courts) has, in recent years, developed a doctrine under which a member of the public (not necessarily the directly aggrieved person) can invoke the court's intervention in a matter of public importance.

When a petition is moved as a PIL, the Court will not insist on procedural formalities. Even the poorest person may, in a simple way, address an application, or just a piece of paper, to the Supreme Court or the High Court concerned, stating the story of the violation of his or any body else's fundamental rights, and the court could treat the application or even the simple piece of paper as a writ petition and proceed according to law.

Officers of the State are answerable to the courts for all their actions and even inaction, which result in perpetration of injustice on individuals and the community at large. The Supreme Court or the High Court concerned could issue appropriate writs to the State and the officers concerned, and also award compensation to the aggrieved person under the Public Law.[vii]

Article 311

All persons under the employ of the Central Government or a State Government, or any of the agencies thereof, are protected against arbitrary removal from service or reduction in rank. Any such action taken against an employee has to be preceded by an inquiry which follows the principle of natural justice based on Article 14, 15, and 21. However, after the inquiry is completed, it is not necessary for the disciplinary authority to issue a second show cause notice to the delinquent on the action proposed to be taken against him (Constitution 42nd Amendment 1976).

An enquiry is not necessary when (1) action is taken after conviction of the delinquent in a criminal case, (2) the disciplinary authority is satisfied that it is not reasonably practicable to hold a enquiry, (3) the President or the Governor concerned is satisfied that it will not be proper to hold an inquiry 'in the interest of the security of the state'. Such satisfaction of the President or a Governor concerned should, however, be based on one or more objective facts, and not on an arbitrary decision of the authorities. An order under the latter two provisions could, therefore, be challenged before an appropriate court.

When a Government servant has been dismissed in contravention of Article 311(1) or 311(2) or a mandatory/statutory rule or the principle of natural justice, he would be entitled to bring a suit against the Government (State of Punjab *vs* Ram, AIR 1992 SC 2188)

In normal cases, the principle of natural justice does not require that the delinquent in an inquiry be assisted by a lawyer. But in certain circumstances, the rules of fairness may ordain that the person charged should get professional help, if he so desires. (IIT *vs* Union of India (1991) Supp 2 SCC12).

In one of the major decisions given by the Supreme Court, it has been laid down that if the misconduct in question is not of 'the gravest kind', the punishment of dismissal would not be appropriate. A minor punishment would be appropriate. A minor punishment would serve the ends of justice in such a case. (State of Punjab *vs* Ram (1992) 4 SCC 54)

It may be noted that a person dismissed becomes ineligible for re-employment under the government while 'removal' does not attach such a disqualification.

In State of Punjab *vs* Sukh Raj, it has been held by the Supreme Court (AIR 1968 SC 1089) that the services of a temporary government servant or a probationer can be terminated under the rules of his employment and such termination will not at attract the operation of Article 311.

Code of Criminal Procedure 1973

As stated earlier, the Police Act 1861 is the legal foundation of the Police in India. The State Police (which include the Police in Union Territories also) are constituted and administered as per its provisions.

However, investigation of crimes being one of the essential functions of the police, which logically involves subsequent prosecution and trial of offenders, it was felt necessary to have a detailed code, which would lay down the working procedures for all the three functions of the justice delivery system. Thus the Code of Criminal Procedure came into being to lay down the procedures not only for police investigations (and the exercise of associate police powers) but also for prosecution and trials and matters relating thereto.[16]

The following are the main points that have found place in the Code of Criminal Procedure 1973 so far as the police are concerned:

1. The Police shall assist the Magistracy including the entire judicial system in the dispensation of justice.
2. It shall have statutory right and duty to investigate cognizable criminal offences without interference.
3. It shall have the power to arrest in order to bring the offenders to justice.
4. It shall have the power and responsibility to use force when necessary to maintain public order.
5. It shall have the power to seize property as required under the provisions of law.
6. It can take preventive actions to thwart commission of crimes by law-breakers in any form.
7. CrPC has made the rank of Sub-Inspector of Police as the cutting edge of the police working system. Though it has not been clearly laid down, a reading of
8. chapter X and XI of the CrPC makes it apparent that it was intended to be as such

16 The CrPC was originally encoded in 1872. It was amended several times in the later years. But the main fault that persisted with the Code was that the functions of the lower judiciary continued to be vested in the hands of the executive. The executive magistrates exercised judicial powers. This was a convenient way for the British colonial power to rule the country comfortably but it naturally led to despotism and arbitrariness. Therefore, in 1973, the new CrPC was enacted with complete separation of powers between the executive and the judiciary. Thus, the judicial system was made independent of the executive at the grassroots level, making the justice delivery system free of bias.

The actual police powers will lie with the officer-in-charge of a police station. The superior police officers having jurisdiction shall be entitled to equivalent powers for better supervision.

Administrative Law

For police officers and men, the principles of Administrative Law are of great consequence. This law is an abstract one, whose principles govern or ought to govern all administrative actions. The common people are almost always at the receiving end of the actions of the police, right or wrong. However, policemen also fall sometimes at to the receiving end of biased and arbitrary actions of their superiors and the Government they serve. The principles of administrative law come here to their help for giving justice to them as much as to the members of the public.

The Constitution of India has ordained that our governance should be based on the principle of rule of law. The concept is totally opposed to the use of any arbitrary power. Rule of law ensures justice for every body, whether rich or poor – powerful or weak. It imposes on the state and all its agencies (including the police) an obligation to perform their duties not only according to the law but also with a fair sense of justice. The Supreme Court has held in Somraj *vs* State of Haryana [(1990) 2 SCC 653] that the first postulate of rule of law is the absence of arbitrary power. It is a basic structure of the Constitution [Keshavananda Bharati *vs* State of Kerala (1973) 4SCC 225].

The Government or its officers take innumerable decisions, which are administrative or quasi-judicial in nature. Such decisions that assail the life of the citizens in one way or the other have to stand the test of fairness and reasonableness if rule of law is to be sustained.

Here comes the principle of natural justice, which follows from the 'higher law of nature' or what may be called 'natural law'. It implies fairness, reasonableness, and equality. It is not the ordinary law of the jungle but one where the lion and the lamb lie together. Natural justice in its turn generates two main principles, viz,

1. No one should be made a judge in his own case. This is rule against 'bias'.
2. The rule of fair hearing should be observed in letter and in spirit, which means that no one should be condemned unheard.

Bias or reasonable suspicion of bias or likelihood of bias is pugnacious to natural justice. In SP Kapoor *vs* State of HP [(1981) 4 SCC 716] the Supreme Court had quashed the selection list made by a Departmental Promotion Committee which had accepted the confidential reports of the candidates prepared by an officer who himself was, at the same time, a candidate for promotion. In another case, a Dy SP, while conducting a departmental enquiry against a constable, made himself a witness in order to contradict a PW's testimony on record. The Supreme Court quashed the proceedings since it was likely that the Enquiry officer was biased against the constable [State of UP *vs* Md Nooh [AIR 1958 SC 86].

Bias could be of the following kinds:

1. Personal bias.
   This arises from personal relationship or equation.
2. Pecuniary bias.
   It may arise from financial interests of the authority concerned.
3. Departmental bias.
   This results from departmental loyalty.
4. Subject matter bias.
   This follows when the deciding officer is involved directly or indirectly with subject of the matter.
5. Pre-conceived bias.
   This results from some preconceived notion.

The rule of fair hearing (audi alteram partem) is the second facet of the law of natural justice. It implies that matters should not be decided unilaterally. It provides for giving a full opportunity to the indicted party to present its own side of the story before a decision is arrived at. In effect it implies that an authority competent to take a penal or disciplinary action must allow the indicted party to inspect all the evidences, be it oral or documentary or in any other form, and to put across its own story *vis a vis* the evidences put forward against it. It will have the right to cross-examine the witnesses to demolish the prosecution story. The entire proceedings have to be transparent so that nothing is done at the back of the party charged for any offence or delinquency.

Ordinarily, there is no statutory requirement for the administrator to give reasons for all his decisions. However when it is a quasi judicial proceedings, there ought to be reasoned decisions and speaking orders which shall state the facts of the case or issue, evidence produced, the defence plea, an assessment of the evidence and the conclusion arrived at with reasons therefor. The entire chain should show procedural fairness in order to stand the test of the principle of natural justice. The breach of the said principle makes the action taken void or void able, in other words, unlawful.

The Protection of Human Rights Act 1993

The Universal Declaration of Human Rights 1948, the International Covenant on Civil and Political Rights 1966 and the International Covenant on Economic, Social and Cultural rights 1966 have already been acceded to by the Government of India. As a follow up to the acceptance of the human rights covenants, the Protection of Human Rights Act 1993 was enacted by the Central Government in India to constitute a National Human Rights Commission (NHRC) at the Centre and a similar Commission in each of the States to go into human rights violations and intervene where necessary.

The National and the State Commissions have been given wide powers under the Act. They may conduct inquiries and investigations independently and recommend action against public servants for illegal omissions and commissions.

Under the Act, there could be separate Human Rights Courts with Special Public Prosecutors appointed for prosecuting human rights violation cases.

In recent times, the said Commissions have taken up *suo motu* the reported violation of human rights at different places in the country. For example, the failure of public officials, including police officials, in Gujarat in protecting the life and properties of the post-Godhra riot victims in 2002 was enquired into by the NHRC. The Assam State Human Rights Commission had even gone into the reports of 'undignified' treatment meted by the police to the bodies of insurgents killed in encounter and issued guidelines to the police to show due respect to dead persons.

Most of the human rights recognised by the international covenants have been incorporated in the Indian Constitution as fundamental rights. Apart from the Human Rights Commissions, there are other statutory bodies, like the National Commission for Minorities, the

National Commission for Women, the National Commission for Protection of Child Rights, etc, which also look after the rights of various segments of the society in their respective fields.

It is therefore important for police officers to remain vigilant about the violation of the rights of the people whether by themselves or by others.

Endnotes

i The discovery in January 2007 of the serial killing of about 30 children, which took place over a period of a year or so at the house of a businessman at Noida (Delhi) and the ham-handed handling of the related kidnapping and murder cases by the police, including their unsympathetic response to the pleadings, from time to time, of the grief-stricken families of the missing children, have been extremely sickening. It was stunningly surprising that the macabre doings of the businessman and his domestic help remained under wraps over such a long time in a high-tech modern city. Obviously, there was not even a semblance of policing in the area. Skeletal remains of many of the murdered children were later recovered from the drains right in front of the slaughterhouse – the residence of the businessman.

Similarly, the 'investigation' by the Noida police into the case of murder on the night of May 15, 2008 of teenager Arushi Talwar and her family's domestic help Hemraj – in which the police initially declared deceased Hemraj as her killer (though his decomposed body lay at the terrace of the scene of crime, only a couple of yards away from that of Arushi) and (later) arrested her grief-stricken father Rajesh Talwar as the prime suspect without a shred of evidence being on record – was, to say the least, horrifying. The press statements of senior police officers given in this regard further added to the horrors of the situation. The later performance of the CBI in the case did not fare any better.

These bizarre incidents – the omissions and commissions of the police (more than the actual acts of crime) – are a matter of deepening concern for the citizens of this country. A natural question that arises is 'do we need such a brand of police at all?'

What had happened in the above two cases was not only the failure of the police but also of the State.

ii The challenges to the security of the state have appeared, among other things, in the form of ethnic insurgencies, Jehadi terrorism and subversion of the economy by way of money-laundering, pumping in of forged currency notes and drug-trafficking. Maoism is the latest addition.

iii The public in India have a common complaint to make that the police are always reluctant to register an FIR (First Information Report) and therefore the victim or the complainant has to run from pillar to post to have his or her complaint recorded for investigation. The police do so apparently to keep the crime record at a low level. But, in this process, they inflict grave injustice on the victims of crime and allow the criminals a free play. The remedy available to the victim in such an event is to approach the Superintendent of Police or the court. But the question is - why should this happen?

iv *The Times of India*, March22, 2009

v *The Sentinel*, December 4, 2005 and *The Telegraph*, January 10, 2006

vi *The Hindu*, February 6, 2006

vii As it generally happens in India, many a good thing tends to be misused by unscrupulous elements for their selfish ends and thereby they nullify the purpose for which it was originally intended. The PIL system, amidst many of its good uses, was also put to grave misuse by fame-seeking people, including lawyers, by invoking the constitutional provision on flimsy excuses. Some of the recorded PIL petitions indeed came to be known as Private Interest Litigations. In order to remedy the situation, the Supreme Court has now asked all the 21 High Courts in the country to admit PILs selectively, 'keeping the focus on those related to the poor, the deprived, the illiterate and the disabled'.

The apex court said that anonymous letters or telegrams should not be treated as PIL. It asserted "PIL is meant for enforcement of fundamental and other legal rights of the people who are poor, weak, ignorant of the legal redressal system, or otherwise in a disadvantageous position due to their social or economic background". "Such litigation can be initiated only for redressal of public injury, enforcement of a public duty or vindicating interest of public nature", it said.

The apex court, however, added that certain types of "private matters" can be treated as PILs, listing for the purpose threats or harassment by private persons, appeal for enquiry by an agency other than the local police, plea for police protection, landlord-tenant dispute, service matters, admission to medical or engineering colleges and request for early hearing of cases.

It further said that issues relating to bonded labour, neglected children, exploitation of casual workers and non-payment of wages to them (except individual cases) and harassment or torture of SCs, STs and the economically backward classes could be taken up as PILs. The other subjects listed by the Supreme Court for entertainment of PIL are environmental pollution, disturbance of ecological balance, drug/food adulteration, maintenance of heritage, antiques, forests and wildlife and petitions from riot victims.

Individual complaints of harassment or torture or death in jail, harassment for dowry, bride burning, rape, complaints relating to family pensions and complaints relating to police refusal to register cases will also come under the ambit of PIL. [The Telegraph, April 20, 2008]

Chapter - II

Important Legal Principles

One of the prime jobs of police officers is to investigate offences committed and to bring the offenders to justice. The Code of Criminal Procedure 1973 provides the framework for investigation, trial, etc. The Evidence Act 1872, as amended up to date, is a statutory guideline regarding admissibility of evidences to regulate investigations by the police and trials in the court, because, after all, it is evidence that proves a person's guilt or innocence.

However, from time to time, the Supreme Court of India (or the High Courts in their respective jurisdiction) lays down certain principles of law on points where the statute or the legislation concerned is silent. Once laid down, these principles acquire the force of law. In this connection, Article 141 of the Constitution is very explicit. It says: "The law declared by the Supreme Court shall be binding on all courts within the territory of India." Our police officers should, therefore, remain acquainted with such newly laid principles to be able to conduct investigations accordingly and establish their cases in the court or even to defend their own rights.

Here are some of the points laid down by the apex court as a lawgiver:

1. Denial of allowance to suspended staff is violation of right to life: SC

In a step to strengthen the right to life under Article 21, the Supreme Court reiterated that a suspended employee couldn't be denied Subsistence Allowance (SA) during pendency of his dispute with the Management.

[*The Times of India*, 25.02.2000]

2. Delhi High Court upholds CAT[1] view

It is a settled position of law that a person cannot hold lien[2] in two permanent posts.

[*The Sentinel* 26.12.1999]

3. Investigation outside jurisdiction

The Supreme Court has ruled that it would be lawful for a police officer to register an FIR and investigate an offence purported to have been committed at a place outside his territorial jurisdiction.

[*The Telegraph* 6.10.1999]

4. More than one FIR for the same offence not valid, rules SC

The Supreme Court has ruled that the sweeping powers given to the police to investigate a case do not empower them to subject citizens to fresh probes in respect of the same offence and file another FIR. Registration of such an FIR would be clearly beyond the purview of sections 154 and 156 of the CrPC and an abuse of power of investigation.

[*The Times of India* 19.7.2001]

5. One agency's case cannot be re-probed by another

In a significant ruling, the Bombay High Court has held that a magistrate or a special court had no powers to order further investigations in a case by another agency. Delivering this verdict, Justice JA Patil held that there was no provision in CrPC, which empowered a magistrate to direct an officer to make further investigation in a case.

Section 173 (3) of CrPC authorised only a superior police officer to direct the O/C of a Police Station to make further investigation. But a magistrate was not empowered to order further probe when already an officer had completed the investigation and filed charge sheet in the same matter.

The right to investigate a cognizable offence is a statutory right of the police and it cannot be interfered with. Ordering further probe would amount to transfer of investigation from one agency to another, which is not permissible in law, the court held.

[*The Times of India*, 20.12.2000]

---

1 Central Administrative Tribunal

2 The right to hold a post after the employee is confirmed in service.

6. *Judicial review can cover departmental proceedings: SC*

In a judgment that would protect innumerable government employees from uncertainty and harassment, the Supreme Court has extended jurisdiction of courts by ruling that availability of judicial review even in case of departmental proceedings cannot be doubted.

Availability of judicial review of administrative actions is a natural requirement for an equitable system and the same has application even in DPs where it is found that the recorded findings are based on no evidence or the findings are totally perverse or legally untenable. The court said it was a fundamental requirement of law that the doctrine of natural justice is complied with in all kinds of proceedings and the same has, as a matter of fact, turned out to be an integral part of administrative jurisprudence in the country.

[*Assam Tribune*, 26.10.2000]

7. *Lifers have no right to go out of prison after 20 years: SC*

Clearing a major misconception, the Supreme Court has held that law does not confer any right on a person serving a sentence for life imprisonment to be released from prison after 20 years of incarceration.

A sentence for life means a sentence for the entire life in prison unless the appropriate government chooses to exercise its discretion to remit either the whole or part of the sentence, a bench of Justice S Rajendra Babu and Justice SN Phukan has said.

Justice Phukan, writing the judgment for the bench, said that the only right the life convict can be said to have acquired was a right to have his case put up in time by the prison authorities before the State Government for consideration of his premature release on some given grounds. They said in considering the case of a life convict, the government would take into consideration the circumstances of the case, character of the crime, his conduct in prison and the probability of his reverting to criminal habits or instigating others to commit crime.

[*Assam Tribune* 18.3.2001]

8. *Anomaly in probe no ground to reject case: SC*

The Supreme Court has said, "There are bound to be some discrepancies between the narrations of different witnesses when they speak on details and unless the contradictions are of material dimension, the same should not be used jettison the evidence entirely".

"Corroboration of evidence with mathematical niceties cannot be expected in criminal cases. Trivial discrepancies ought not obliterate an otherwise acceptable evidence."

[*The Sentinel* 13.10.1999]

9. Circumstantial evidence should have an unbroken chain

Guilt must be proved beyond doubt. Where a case rests on circumstantial evidence, such evidence must be cogently and firmly established. The circumstances must form a chain pointing towards the guilt of the accused and the condition that within human probability, the crime was committed by him and none else. [Additional Sessions Judge GP Thanja of Delhi said this in his order acquitting the accused in Priyadarshini Mattoo case. The judge said that due to the goof-up in the investigation, the accused (a senior police officer's son), though not innocent, had to be acquitted as the chain of the circumstances of the incident of murder was broken giving benefit to the accused.[3]

10. SC interprets right to equality in new light

The concept of equality before law does not involve the idea of absolute equality among human beings, which is a physical impossibility. All that Article 14 of the Constitution guarantees is a similarity of treatment contra-distinguished from identical treatment.

[*The Times of India*, 11.1.2001]

11. Magistrate has no power to direct CBI to probe an offence: SC

A division bench comprising Justice KT Thomas and Justice RP Sethi said that a magistrate could only direct an officer in charge of a local police station to probe a case.

Under the provision of law, magisterial power cannot be extended beyond "directing the officer-in-charge of a police station to conduct the investigation".

The bench also made it clear that the magistrate could not direct a police officer above the rank of an officer-in-charge (of a police

---

3 Thanks to a strong public agitation on the outcome of the gory rape-cum-murder case, the Delhi High Court took up the State's appeal against the judgment on a priority basis and made an appreciation of the circumstantial evidence put up by the police. The accused in the case has since been sentenced to death by the High Court.

station) to conduct investigation, though a superior police officer could exercise his power to conduct investigation into the same case.

[*The Sentinel*, 18.1.2001]

12. Employer has the right to terminate service of a probationer: SC

The Supreme Court has ruled that an employer has the right to terminate during probation period a person's services when not found to be satisfactory.

[*The Sentinel*, 18.1.2001]

13. Judge granting bail should also hear plea for its cancellation: SC

The Supreme Court has ordered that if a judge in the first instance grants bail to an accused and the State felt that the order was obtained by misrepresentation of facts, an application for cancellation of the bail should be placed before the same judge and none else.

[*NE Times* 10.12.01]

14. SC opinion on 'dying declaration'

A dying declaration, if found reliable, could form the basis of conviction. However, it stands on the same footing as any other piece of evidence. It has to be judged and appreciated in the light of surrounding circumstances and its weight determined by reference to principles governing the weighing of evidence.

First, if it suffers from any infirmities, either of its own or as disclosed by other evidence, the court might, as a rule of prudence, look for corroboration. (Justice RC Lahoti and Justice D Raju)

[*The Telegraph* 20.10.1999]

Second, two dying declarations voluntarily made to two different persons at different points of time can be the basis of conviction of an accused if they corroborate each other. (Bench headed by Justice GB Pattanaik)

[*The Telegraph* 20.10.1999]

Third, section 32(i) of the Evidence Act made two categories of dying declarations admissible in evidence and further made them substantive evidence. Justice KT Thomas said "they are his statement as to the cause of death and his statement as to any of the circumstances of the transaction which resulted in his death." Anything which has a nexus with his death, proximate or distant, direct or indirect, can also fall within the purview of the sub-section."

The court, however, has to consider if the dying declaration is reliable, keeping in mind the attendant circumstances. It is therefore required of the investigating officer to deeply probe the attendant circumstances of an unnatural death in which a dying declaration has been given.

[*The Sentinel*, 20.10.2001]

15. Conviction of co-accused u/s 34 IPC

The offence u/s 34 IPC was intended to meet a situation wherein all the co-accused had done something to constitute the criminal act, a Supreme Court bench headed by Justice KT Thomas said.

To attract section 34, two postulates were indispensable:

First, the criminal act (consisting of a series of acts) should have been done by more than one person.

Second, doing of such individual acts cumulatively resulting in the commission of the criminal offence should have been in furtherance of common intention of all such persons.

On the first postulate, the bench said, 'the accused who is to be fastened with the liability on the strength of section 34 IPC should have done some act which has a nexus with the offence. Such an act need not be substantial; it is enough that the act was only for guarding the scene for facilitating the crime.'

'It is however difficult to conclude that a person, merely because he was present at or near the scene of crime, without doing anything more, without even carrying a weapon, without even marching along with other assailants, could be convicted with the aid of section 34 for the offence committed by others.'

[*The Times of India*, 4.3.2001]

16. Compensation for helping police

The Bombay High Court has ordered the Maharashtra Government to pay a compensation of Rs 3 lakh to the widow of a person who was killed while helping the police apprehend criminals. The judges observed that it was the State's duty to maintain law and order through the police and when a policemen directs a person to apprehend suspected criminals, the State should pay compensation in the event of his death.

[*The Telegraph*, 22.3.2001]

17. Married woman not a member of the parents' family.

The Supreme Court has ruled that a married woman, even if she is staying with her parents due to special circumstances, cannot be counted as a member of her parents' family.

[*PTI*, 21.4.2001]

18. Sole testimony of rape victims must be reliable to be accepted: SC

The Supreme Court has held that the sole testimony of a victim of a sexual offence can be the basis for conviction provided it is safe, reliable and worthy of acceptance.

It is time that the evidence of the prosecutrix in a rape case is given due weight. Sexual violence is a dehumanising act and an unlawful encroachment into the right of privacy and sanctity of a woman.

It is however equally important that there must be fairness to all sides.

[*The NE Times*, 25.12.2002]

19. Benefit of doubt in murder case

Laying down guidelines for courts on the grant of the benefit of doubt in murder cases, the Supreme Court has said that a reasonable doubt is not an imaginary, trivial or merely possible doubt but a firm doubt based on reason and common sense.

Proof beyond doubt is a guideline and not a fetish. A judge does not preside over a criminal trial merely to see that no innocent man is punished. He has also to see that the guilty man does not escape. Both are public duties.

[*The NE Times*, 14.10.2002]

20. Common object can be inferred in a preplanned attack: SC

There may not be a common object in a sudden fight but in a planned attack on the victim, the presence of the common object amongst persons forming an unlawful assembly can be inferred, a bench comprising Justice RP Sethi and Justice D Ranju said.

The bench gave the ruling while dismissing the appeals of accused persons charged with murdering six persons of a family in Bihar 1994. It was alleged by the prosecution that around 300 to 400 person raided the house of one Bholi Singh and shot him dead and burnt alive the others. The mob also fired 300 – 400 rounds at the house. The police charge sheeted 19 persons.

The accused pleaded they were only bystanders and had not actually committed the crime. They also contended the prosecution had failed to establish existence of common object amongst the accused persons.

Rejecting the contention Justice Sethi writing for the bench said, "When a concerted attack is made by a large number of persons, it is rather difficult to determine the actual part played by each of the accused".

[*The Sentinel*, 18.04.2002]

21. 'Admission' is the best evidence: SC

A bus conductor was found collecting money from passengers and not issuing tickets. He admitted his guilt. Reference was made to the Industrial Tribunal concerned under Industrial Disputes Act for approval of the order of his removal from service. The tribunal rejected the order saying that the 'admission' by the conductor was of no consequence.

The Supreme Court disagreed with the view and held that admission was the best evidence. The persons making the admission may be asked to explain why the statement should not be acted upon.

[*The Telegraph*, 13.10.2004]

22. Cop registering FIR can also investigate the case: SC

A bench comprising Justice Ruma Paul and Justice PV Reddi said in a judgment that it was not proper to lay a broad and unqualified proposition that investigation would necessarily be unfair or biased if it was undertaken by the officer who records the FIR. The bench said, the formality of preparing the FIR and then taking up investigation did not vitiate the investigation on the ground of bias or like factor.

[*UNI*, 05.04.04]

23. SC against spiking half true statements

The Supreme Court has ruled that the statement of a witness cannot be discarded totally by the trial court merely because it was found to be false in certain aspects. The apex court said, the maxim 'false in one thing, false in everything' (*falsus uno falsus omnibus*) has no applicability in India. Witnesses cannot be branded as total liars.

[*The Telegraph*, 22.10.02]

24. Questioning a dog's nose

The Supreme Court has held that if a police dog led to an accused and he was caught, it could not be taken as evidence of his committing the crime. The court lauded certain breeds of dogs, which have the ability to sniff and track culprits but pointed out that there was a possibility of error on the part of the dog or its handlers. There was also a possibility of a misrepresentation of or a wrong inference from the behaviour of the dog. From a scientific point of view, there was little knowledge and much uncertainty as to the precise faculties, which enable police dogs to track and identity criminals.

The bench comprising Justice KT Thomas and Justice RP Sethi added that dogs provided valuable clues with the right training but the clues in themselves were not evidence.

[*The Times of India*, 11.07.2001]

25. Evidence can be recorded via video-conferencing: SC

The Supreme Court has upheld the recording of deposition through video conferencing. The judgment came after a Mumbai trial court had allowed video-conferencing of US doctor Ernest Greenbeng, who was unable to come to India to depose in a case. He had given an opinion against operating on a woman cancer patient but ignoring the advice, two Indian doctors had operated on her leading to her death.

Her husband PC Singhi and the Maharashtra Government had appealed to the SC against the Bombay High Court order disallowing video-conferencing.

The Supreme Court held that such video conferencing would be legal. Where the attendance of the witness cannot be procured without (unusual) delay, expenses or inconvenience, the court could consider issuing a commission to record evidence by way of video-conferencing.

However, 'evidence by video-conferencing in an open court should be taken only if the witness is in a country which has extradition treaty (with India) and under whose laws contempt of court and perjury are also punishable'.

[*The Times of India*, 03.04.03]

26. SC nod to arrest of women without woman cop

The Supreme Court has ruled that a woman accused could be arrested without a woman constable being present but only in certain circumstances. The court emphasized that all efforts should be made to keep a lady constable present.

But in certain circumstances where the arresting officer is reasonably satisfied that a lady constable is not immediately available and to secure the presence of such a constable is not immediately possible while the delay in arrest would impede the investigation, a woman accused could be arrested without the presence of a lady constable.

[*The Telegraph*, 17.10.2003]

27. Conviction for offence u/s 376 IPC

The Supreme Court has ruled that the sole testimony of the victim would suffice for conviction in a rape case. The testimony of the victim in such cases is vital and unless there are compelling reasons which necessitate looking for corroboration of her statement, the courts should find no difficulty to act on the testimony of a victim of sexual assault alone where her testimony inspires confidence and is found to be reliable.

In 1989, an 18-year-old boy raped an 8-year-old girl in a Rajasthan village. The accused was convicted and sentenced by the trial court to 7 years of rigorous imprisonment. The High Court refused to believe the testimony of the child victim and acquitted the accused. The State then moved the Supreme Court against the acquittal. The apex court said, 'seeking corroboration of her statement amounted to adding insult to the injury and such cases needed a sensitive approach since the victim carried the scars of the crime for her entire life time'.

[*The Telegraph*, 06.05.2002]

Some Railway employees at Howrah Station raped Hanuffa Khatoon, a citizen of Bangladesh, in 1998. The Supreme Court, while asking the Railways to pay her compensation, for the first time declared rape to be a violation of the fundamental right to live with dignity under the Indian Constitution and the Universal Declaration of Human Rights 1948.

The testimony of a child who had been subjected to sexual assault should be recorded at the earliest opportunity by a magistrate in presence of a friend, relative or social worker whom the minor trusts. While recording evidence of the minor, appropriate breaks should be given to make the minor feel comfortable.

[172nd Report of the Law Commission of India]

28. Vicarious liability for commission of a crime with common object

The Supreme Court has held that each member of an unlawful assembly will be held vicariously liable for the crime committed by any member of such assembly if it is found that the offence was committed in pursuance of a common object.

The court, however, said that if the offence was committed by a few members of the unlawful assembly on certain provocation at the scene of crime, members who did not participate in committing the crime would not be liable vicariously.

[*The Telegraph*, 01.12.2001]

29. More papers can be filed after submission of charge sheet: SC

Strengthening the hands of investigating agencies, particularly those dealing with complex cases, the Supreme Court has ruled that they could file additional documents before the trial court even after the submission of the charge sheet.

Giving the judgment which may have bearing on the Bofors and the Securities scam cases, the court said that though the investigating official was required to produce all the relevant documents at the time of submitting the charge sheet, there was no specific prohibition against filing additional documents during the trial.

'If some mistake is committed in not producing the relevant documents at the time of filing the charge sheet, it is always open to the I/O to produce the same later with the permission of the court'.

[*The Times of India*, 05.04.2002]

30. Foreigner on voters list can't claim citizenship: SC

A division bench of the Supreme Court comprising Justice D Raju and Justice A Bhan ruled that a foreigner couldn't be granted Indian citizenship even though, per chance, he may have been enlisted as a voter.

Long stay in the country and enrolment in the voters' list does not confer any right to an alien to stay in the country, the court said while rejecting the plea of Pakistani national Bhanwaroo Khan (70) who was seeking citizenship for his wife on the ground that they had been staying in India since 1955.

[*The Times of India*, 05.04.2002]

31. First informant investigating a case is bad law.

If the complainant in a case who files the FIR is a police officer, he sometimes proceeds to investigate the case himself for reasons not stated. Though such an investigation is not illegal, it is bad in law.

[Megha Singh *vs* State of Haryana (SC) AIR 1995;

Shibjoy Reang *vs* State of Tripura, Guwahati High Court 2000]

32. Right to information is a fundamental right

In 2004, the Supreme Court passed a judgment in the case 'Peoples Union for Civil Liberties *vs* Union of India', which stated that the right to information is a fundamental right.

[*The Telegraph*, 23.02.2005]

33. Disposal of seized property.

Powers under section 451 CrPC for disposal of seized property in cases pending trial should be exercised by the court concerned expeditiously and judiciously.

Seized articles should not be kept at police stations for a long time, said the Supreme Court.

[SC 638 AIR 2003]

34. Back wages

The Supreme Court has held that if a court reinstates an employee setting aside an earlier order of his dismissal, it would not be mandatory for the employer to pay him *back wages* in full for the impugned period.

[*Hindustan Times*, 15.07.2003]

35. Circumstantial evidence

When circumstances point to the accused as the possible assailant and he offers no explanation, which, if accepted though not proved, would afford a reasonable basis for a conclusion on the entire case consistent with his innocence, such absence of explanation or false explanation would itself be an additional link which completes the chain.

[Deonandan Mishra *vs* State of Bihar, 1965 CLJ 1647]

36. Dying declaration

When an FIR clearly implicating the accused and giving details of the incident was lodged by the deceased, it was held that the same could be used as a dying declaration.

37. Sample of Blood

No one can be compelled to give sample of blood for analysis.

[Gautam Khandu *vs* State of West Bengal SC 2295 – AIR 1993]

38. Offence under Prevention of Corruption Act

A public servant cannot be convicted for the offence of taking illegal gratification under the Prevention of Corruption Act unless there is evidence to the effect that he had demanded money. Thus, held the Supreme Court in 'Subhas Parbat Sonvane *vs* State of Gujarat'.

[*The Telegraph*, 22.05.2002]

39. Guidelines for Bail

Observing that an order of bail bereft of any cogent reason could not be sustained, the Supreme Court laid down the following guidelines for trial courts and High Courts for granting bail to the accused.

(a) The nature of the offence is one of the basic considerations; the more heinous is the crime, the greater is the chance for rejection of the bail. Much depends on the factual matrix of the matter.

(b) Severity of the punishment laid down in the law.

(c) Apprehension of witness being influenced and evidence being tampered with.

(d) Threat to the complainant/witness.

(e) Possibility of frivolous cases being initiated.

(f) Though courts should protect an individual's liberty by ordinarily granting bail, they should keep in mind that in case of a commission of a heinous offence, it was the society, which needed protection from elements committing crimes.

[*The Telegraph*, 21.03.2002]

40. SC verdict in favour of 'first wife'

In an important order relating to matrimonial law, the Supreme Court has ruled that only the legally married wife and not the woman who is treated or kept like one, is entitled to get maintenance from the husband. The second wife who cannot be legally called a wife cannot have a valid claim for maintenance, the bench comprising Justice A Pasayat and Justice SH Kapadia said. However, the court upheld the claim of the child 'born out of the second marriage for maintenance'.[4]

[*The Sentinel*, 14.03.2005]

41. Cruelty to wife defined

Expanding the definition of cruelty in marital discords, the Supreme Court has ruled that abnormal behaviour of a husband causing mental agony to the wife is an act of cruelty for which he can be convicted. A bench comprising Justice RP Sethi and Justice BP Singh said that cruelty need not always be physical. Its effect varies from person to person and also depends upon the social and economic status to which such persons belong.

[*The Times of India*, 08.02.2002]

The apex court has further said that mental cruelty[5] consists of one or more of the following ingredients:

- Withholding sex without reason,
- Unilateral decision not to have a child,
- Abortion or sterilization without the consent of spouse,

---

4 Of late, this approach has increasingly been undergoing a change. Now, the right of a live-in partner to maintenance and to live in the same household has been recognised under the Protection of Women from Domestic Violence Act 2005.

5 46 per cent of divorce cases in India are filed on the ground of mental cruelty. [*India Today*, April 16, 2007]

- Nagging behaviour,
- Indifference and frigidity,
- Denial of company,
- Filthy language and verbal abuse,
- False allegations.

[*India Today*, 16. 04. 2007]

The Telegraph (March 31, 2007) editorially commented that to lay down specifically what constitutes mental cruelty within marriage might be fraught with risks and ambiguities.

42. Wear and tear of matrimonial life not cruelty

The Delhi High Court has held that normal instances of 'wear and tear' of matrimonial life would certainly not constitute a cruel conduct. Justice Madan Lokur held that on the basis of various judgments of the Supreme Court, it could be said that for the conduct of a spouse to amount to cruelty, it should be such as to make it virtually impossible for the other spouse to enjoy a healthy and normal life. The Court said, 'cruelty can be said to be an act committed with the intention to cause sufferings to the opposite party. Severity of temper, rudeness of language, occasional outburst of anger may not amount to cruelty though it may amount to misconduct. One has to look at the overall conduct of the parties and take their sensibilities and sensitivities into account. Even an act or two may amount to cruelty if it results in an apprehension of a spouse that it is not possible to maintain a conducive matrimonial home.' The apex court, however, has emphasised the need to distinguish it from normal wear and tear of matrimonial life, the judge said.

[*UNI*, 6.9.2004]

43. Corroboration of confession

In a controversial judgment, the Supreme Court upheld the death sentence for Depender Pal Singh who had killed nine persons while making an attempt to eliminate Congress leader MS Bitta in a bomb explosion. The majority judgment said that even though the prosecution had failed to corroborate the evidence of the accused confessing the crime, it could not be a ground for acquitting him. Any compassion for such persons would frustrate the purpose of enactment of the TADA (P) Act and would amount to unwarranted sympathy, the court said.

If, however, there is a difference of opinion in the bench over a death sentence, the necessity to implement the extreme penalty on someone who had committed a heinous crime becomes debatable.

[*The Times of India*, 17.6.2002 and 23.12.2002]

Justice PN Bhagwati had, after a detailed study, said that in India, only the poor were sent to the gallows.

43A. Police cannot hound innocent people: SC

In a significant ruling the Supreme Court said that the police or the CBI couldn't hound people merely to ascertain if they had committed an offence. Right to life means more than mere survival or animal existence. A man has, therefore, to be left alone to enjoy life without fetters. Legal experts said the court's ruling on Article 21 should be treated as a caution to the investigating agencies, which are known to hound victims of crime in order to shield the perpetrators.

[*The Times of India*, 4.8.1999]

44. Right of private defence

The Supreme Court has let off two persons for inflicting injuries on their tormentors, ruling that right to self-defence should be liberally construed.

'Law does not require a person, whose property is forcibly tried to be occupied by trespassers, to run away and seek protection of the authorities'.

'The right of private defence serves a social purpose and that right should be liberally construed. Such a right will be a restraining influence on bad characters and it will encourage the right spirit in a free citizen'.

Subramani, a resident of Tamil Nadu, and a few others had resisted a group of people, who had come to grab their land. Several of the aggressors were seriously injured in the clash. The Madras High Court convicted Subramani and others for causing grievous hurt.

The Supreme Court ruled that Subramani and his friends were assaulted by the aggressors and in self-defence the appellants had to hit back without exceeding the right of self-defence. The circumstances of the case showed that the exercise of the right of private defence was inevitable, the court said.

[*The Telegraph*, 29.8.2002]

45. Private parties can move SC to prevent miscarriage of justice

In a criminal case, persons other than the State and the accused have ordinarily no *locus standi* to file an appeal. However, a bench comprising Justice D Raju and Justice A Pasayat said that an interested private party apprehending miscarriage of justice could move a petition to the Supreme Court under Article 136 of the Constitution.

The ruling came in a murder case in which the trial court had convicted four persons on various charges. However, the Allahabad High Court acquitted all the accused. The father of the victim then moved the Supreme Court challenging the acquittal but the accused questioned his *locus standi.*

[*The Times of India*, 24.10.2004]

46. Confession no breather: SC

The Supreme Court has held that the confession made by an accused (of having committed the crime in question) is no legal ground for the court to reduce the sentence awarded to him.

[*The Telegraph*, 3.11.1999]

47. Dying declaration is not the sole proof: SC

A dying declaration is an independent piece of evidence like any other piece of evidence – neither extra strong nor too weak – and can be acted upon without corroboration if it is found otherwise free and reliable. Thus ruled a division bench comprising Justice KT Thomas and Justice DP Wadhwa. It said that the person making a dying declaration should have had the opportunity to identify the person implicated before the same could be accepted as a strong piece of evidence.

[*The Times of India*, 30.9.1999]

48. Lie detector findings crucial

The polygraph test, which is purportedly used for detecting lies being told by a person during his or her interrogation, is based on a scientific theory that lying is accompanied by specific and noticeable physical and behavioural charges such as tension, agitation, changes in respiration, etc. It is not admissible in law as evidence but helpful in detection of a crime.

Though courts cannot rely on the findings of a polygraph test, a Calcutta court had drawn an adverse inference against some Punjab police officials including IPS officers, who were charged with the murder of a couple suspected to be militants. The police officers were charged for the Tiljala double murder case but had refused to take the polygraph test.

[*The Times of India*, 29.9.2003]

49. Torture in Custody

No circumstance can justify the use of torture. Neither war, nor insurgency, nor public emergency, nor orders from superiors can be invoked to explain away the practice. It is forbidden by the Constitution as also by various rulings of the Supreme Court. It is forbidden absolutely under international humanitarian laws and the human rights instruments of the United Nations. [NHRC]

[*The Times of India*, 26.6.2000]

50. Children from second marriage have right to property

The Supreme Court has ruled that the children of a Hindu father born out of his illegal second marriage, even though his first marriage was subsisting, were entitled to equal share in the property and assets left behind by him.

The second wife of the void marriage, however, would not be entitled to any share in the property, pension and gratuity on the death of her husband, it said.

51. Prosecution case based on evidence cannot fail for want of motive: SC

The Supreme Court has ruled that a murder case based on direct evidence cannot and does not become weak for apparent absence of motive. Setting aside Allahabad High Court's acquittal of a man accused of murdering his father, mother and brother, the court said that the prosecution's failure to establish the motive does not weaken the case.

If the prosecution proved the motive, it would be well and good, particularly in a case that depends on circumstantial evidence, for such motive could then be counted as one of the circumstances, the court said.

[*The Times of India*, 15.4.2000]

52. SC against roping in all in-laws in dowry cases

The Supreme Court has expressed strong reservations against the practice of the police to file, on the basis of allegations of the parents of the deceased, charges against all the in-laws of the victim in dowry death cases. 'A tendency has developed for roping in all relations (related to the husband) and in-laws of the deceased in matters of dowry deaths, which, if not discouraged, is likely to affect the case of the prosecution even against the real culprits', the court said.

The bench comprising Justice GB Pattanaik, Justice RP Sethi and Justice SV Patil said that in cases where accusations were made against all and sundry, the overt acts attributed to persons were required to be proved beyond all reasonable doubts.

[*The Times of India*, 5.6.2000]

53. Illegitimate child

An illegitimate child is also entitled to maintenance, observed the Supreme Court (in DP Satpathy *vs* BP Dixit and another). The court rejected the contention of the husband who tried to disown his marriage alleging he was pushed into it at knife point. The apex court held that in a proceeding u/s 125 CrPC, if the claimant could establish that she lived together with the man concerned as his wife, the court will presume that they were legally married spouses and the husband will be obliged to support the wife and the child.

[*The Telegraph*, 24.4.1999]

54. Scheduled Tribes are exempted from application of Section 494 IPC for bigamy: Delhi High Court

Bigamy is an offence u/s 494 IPC punishable with seven years of imprisonment. But this penal provision will not apply if the offender is a member of a Scheduled Tribes.

[*The Sentinel*, 13.4.2000]

55. Curative petition

A person who loses his last battle at the Supreme Court has sometimes to live with the grievance that gross injustice had been done to him but he has no further remedy. With a view to offering another opportunity to such genuinely aggrieved persons, a bench of the apex court headed by Chief Justice SP Bharucha offered a solution – a curative petition.

A curative petition can be accepted for fresh hearing if a petitioner can show that the principle of natural justice – the right to be heard – had been violated, as he – the affected person – was not served notice or not heard during the proceedings. Secondly, the judge hearing the petition had failed to disclose his own connection, if any, with the subject matter or the parties concerned. This gave scope for an apprehension of bias and the judgement affected the petitioner.

All the grounds stated in the review petition must be incorporated in the curative petition, which must be certified by a senior advocate. The curative petition would first be circulated to a bench of three seniormost judges and the judges who had passed the earlier judgment, if available. Only when the majority of the judges on this combined bench will conclude that the plea needs hearing, it should be listed before the same bench for appropriate order.

The bench may at any stage ask a senior advocate to assist it as *amicus curie*. If at any stage the court finds that the curative petition lacks merits and was vexatious, it can impose exemplary cost on the petitioner.

[*The Times of India*, 15. 04. 2002]

56. Nagging and divorce

In a widely discussed judgment, the Supreme Court has held that a husband, who is subjected to abuse, humiliation and emotional trauma by his wife, is entitled to seek divorce on the ground of constant nagging. However, nagging should be of extreme nature and more serious than the ordinary wear and tear of married life.

The case was that of a pair of doctors who got married in 1978. The husband was a Telegu Brahmin and the wife a Sikh. They have two children. After nineteen years of marriage, the husband sought divorce on the ground of cruelty, which the court granted after a long battle.

57. SC guidelines on court proceedings in child sexual abuse case

(i) A screen or some other arrangement must be in place so that the victim and the witness do not have to see the face or body of the accused during trial.

(ii) The defence counsel is barred from asking direct questions. The questions must be written and handed out to the judge who would then address them to the victim in clear but not embarrassing language.

(iii) The victim may be given as many breaks as necessary.

[*The Telegraph*, 30.05.2004]

58. Common intention

In a quarrel arising over the cleaning of a drain, five accused persons entered the victim's house and beat her up. They were charged under several provisions of the Indian Penal Code, including Section 34. Acquitting the accused the High Court held that in order to prove common intention, the prosecution must establish that the attack was pre-conceived. However, the Supreme held that when the five had barged into the house and beaten her up, it was clear that there was a common intention. [State of Maharashtra *vs* Jagmohan and Kuldip Singh]

59. Right to strike

Government employees have no 'fundamental, legal, moral or equitable right to go on strike even for a just cause', said the Supreme Court. The Court further maintained that 'no political party or organisation can claim a right to paralyse the economic and industrial activities of a state or the nation or cause inconvenience to the citizens. In the case of strike by teachers, the entire educational system suffers; in case of strike by doctors, innocent patients suffer; if transport employees go on strike, the movements of the entire society come to a standstill'.

[*The Sentinel*, 23.08.2003]

60. Medical proof vital in criminal case

The Supreme Court has ruled that in murder cases where direct evidence is scanty, medical evidence has a vital role. The trial court can convict an accused on the basis of a circumstantial evidence, provided it was so complete as to leave no doubt about the guilt of the accused. When the prosecution case was mainly based on circumstantial evidence, medical evidence plays an important role, said a bench comprising Justice KT Thomas and Justice RP Shetty. The chain of circumstances furnished by the prosecution should be so complete as not to lead to any reasonable ground for conclusion consistent with innocence of the accused. The court cited the oft-quoted proverb 'witness may lie but the circumstances cannot.'

The judgment followed an appeal relating to the murder of one Roop Devi, who was married to one Shyam Mohan in June 1973. On receipt of a letter from her, her father had gone to see her on March 18, 1977 when his son-in-law's brother told him that she had died of cholera a few days back. Suspecting foul play, her father lodged an FIR and after two days, her bullet-ridden body was recovered. The trial court convicted the accused with life imprisonment but the High Court acquitted him, whereupon the State went up in appeal to the Supreme Court. The apex court reversed the High Court order on the basis of circumstantial evidence in the case.

[*The Times of India*, 18.11.2000]

61. Retraction of a confession does not make it wholly inadmissible: SC

In a major ruling, the Supreme Court has held that retraction of a confession by an accused does not render the confessional statement wholly inadmissible though the courts have to be careful in evaluating the same. It is not the law that once retracted, a confession becomes tainted, the bench comprising Justice KT Thomas and Justice S.N.Vairava said in a judgment.

The ruling came in the case of the murder of 'the dainty film actress of the South' Rani Padmini and her mother Indrani Kumari in Chennai more than 15 years ago. Though the trial court had convicted their driver, watchman and cook and sentenced them to death, the High Court acquitted the watchman and the cook and altered the sentence of the driver to life imprisonment. On an appeal by the State of Tamilnadu, the Supreme Court restored the conviction but imposed life imprisonment on all the three.

The apex court further said that the twin test of a confession is to ascertain whether it was made voluntarily and whether it was true. Non-retracted confession is rare in criminal cases. Referring to the case on hand, the court questioned the High Court finding that the judicial confession was bad as the articles belonging to the victims were recovered prior to the making of the confession. That aspect, instead of vitiating the confession, could be a factor in favour of the voluntariness of the confession. When the culprit found that the articles were recovered, it was possible he might have felt that there was no use in concealing the facts any more, the apex court added. Convicting all the three, the bench said, "We cannot overlook the sturdy evidence of the investigating officer who effected the recovery and that evidence is supported by documents contemporaneously prepared by him to prove the case."

[*PTI* 16.08.2001]

62. Horoscope can't certify age: SC

The Supreme Court has held that the date recorded in a horoscope cannot be taken as a conclusive proof for determining the age of a person.

The school records have more probative value than a horoscope for determining the exact date of birth, the court said. It, however, added that where no other material is available, the horoscope might be considered but its authenticity has to be established. For a horoscope to be treated as an evidence in terms of Section 32 (5) of the Indian Evidence Act, it must be proved to have been prepared by a person having special knowledge regarding the authenticity of date and time mentioned therein, a bench comprising Justice A Pasayat and Justice SH Kapadia said.

63. Railways under Motor Vehicles Act

It has been held by the Supreme Court that the Railways will have to pay compensation according to the provisions of MV Act in case of an accident with a motor vehicle. A three-judge bench of the apex court comprising Justice GB Pattanaik, Justice S.N.Phukan and Justice S.N.Vairava rejected the plea of the Railways that an Accident Claims Tribunal under the MV Act did not have the power to direct it to pay compensation to the relatives of accident victims.

The court held that if a motor vehicle was involved in an accident with a train, the jurisdiction of the tribunal could not be ousted.

[*The Telegraph*, 22.04.2003]

64. Self defence plea of an accused depends on evidence: SC

The Supreme Court has ruled that the right of private defence is related to the following factors, *viz*:

(a) The injuries received by the accused;

(b) The imminence of threat to his safety;

(c) The injuries caused by the accused;

(d) The circumstances whether the accused had time to have recourse to public authorities.

In order to find whether the right of private defence is available to an accused person, the entire incident will have to be examined with care and viewed in a proper setting, the court said.

[*NE Times*, 10.10.2002]

65. Magistrate can only ask OC to probe case: Calcutta High Court

No magistrate can direct any police officer other than an officer-in-charge of a police station of the area concerned to investigate a case, ruled the Calcutta High Court citing a Supreme Court directive in 'CBI *vs* State of Rajasthan (2001)'.

Setting aside an order (February, 2002) of the Sub-Divisional Magistrate, Barrackpore, directing the DIG, CID to investigate a case, the High Court ordered that the case in question would now be shifted to the O/c of the Police Station concerned for taking necessary steps.

[*The Times of India*, 19.04.2003]

66. Sole testimony of rape victim must be reliable to be accepted: SC

The Supreme Court has held that the sole testimony of a victim of sexual offence can be a basis for conviction provided it is safe, reliable and worthy of acceptance. Applying this principle, the court acquitted an accused charged with the offence of rape, giving him the benefit of doubt.

The court said, 'it is true that the evidence of the prosecutrix in a rape case is to be given due weight. But it is equally important that there is fairness to all sides'.

[*NE Times*, 25.12.2002]

67. Child witness can be relied upon

The Supreme Court has ruled that the testimony of a child witness in a criminal case cannot be rejected outright, but may be scrutinised with care and caution. Some small discrepancies in the statement of a child witness should not be the reason to discard the testimony. However, while evaluating a child's statement, the courts are required to examine the possibility of the child having been tutored. The apex court said that the corroboration of the testimony of a child witness is not a rule but a measure of caution and prudence.

A bench comprising Justices KT Thomas and Justice RP Sethi upheld a Karnataka High Court judgment, which had confirmed the conviction and sentence of life imprisonment awarded to a murder accused on the evidence of a four-year-old girl child.

[*The Times of India*, 06.01.2001]

68. Evidence of a hostile witness can be relied upon: SC

The Supreme Court has held that merely because a witness had turned hostile, his entire testimony cannot become unworthy of consideration by the trial court. A bench consisting of Justices KT Thomas and RP Sethi said that it was for the trial court to decide on the basis of cross-examination of the hostile witness as to which part of the testimony is to be relied upon.

69. Extra-judicial confession

One Gura Singh, after killing his father on a trivial issue, had made an extra-judicial confession to two persons, one of whom filed the FIR before the police. The accused pleaded innocence.

The Supreme Court upheld the trial court view that extra-judicial confession, if true and voluntary, could be relied upon to convict the accused for the commission of the crime alleged.

However, the weight of such a confession would depend on the circumstances of the case, the time when the confession was made and the credibility of the witness before whom such confession was made. The witness before whom such statement was made should not have had any reason to state anything falsely to implicate the accused.

Justice Sethi said that retraction of extra-judicial confession, which is a usual phenomenon in criminal cases, would by itself not weaken the case of prosecution based upon such confession.

[*NE Times*, 08.12.2000]

70. A company director can be prosecuted if his company's cheques bounce

In a judgment of far reaching consequence, the Supreme Court has said that in the case of a bounced cheque, there is no bar for proceeding against everyone responsible for the business of the company concerned, including a director, a secretary or any officer of the company. Till now, only the person signing the cheque and the company were held responsible for bouncing of cheque under the Negotiable Instruments Act.

The Court said that under Section 141 of the NI Act, three categories of persons could be brought under the purview of penal liability, *viz*,

(a) The company, which committed the offence;

(b) Anyone in charge of and responsible for its business affairs;

(c) Any other person, who is a director, a manager, a secretary or an officer of the company.

[*The Telegraph*, 30.11.1999]

71. Tribal won't lose ST status even after conversion

The Supreme Court has ruled that a tribal, even after conversion to some other religion, would not lose his Scheduled Tribe status unless it is shown that he has given up his tribal customs and been only practising those of the adopted religion.

The judgment by a bench comprising Chief Justices VN Khare, Justice SB Sinha and Justice SH Kapadia came in an unusual case where a person accused of outraging modesty of an ST girl questioned the police decision to charge him with an offence under the SC and ST (Prevention of Atrocities) Act 1989. The accused contended that the girl's family had converted to Christianity around 200 hundred years back and were not following tribal customs. Here they could not be classified as tribal, he alleged.

[*PTI*, 04.02.2004]

72. Prosecutor alone can select witness

The Supreme Court has underscored the Public Prosecutor's discretion in producing witnesses during the trial of a case. A bench of Justice D Raju and Justice A Pasayat said that without impairing the cause of justice, a limited number of witnesses should be cited by the prosecution to avoid the waste of time of the courts in recording the same story repeatedly.

[*The Times of India*, 07.11.2003]

73. Sex under fear is rape: SC

Submission of her body under fear or terror cannot be construed as consent for sex, ruled the Supreme Court widening the definition of rape under section 375 of IPC. Quashing the acquittal by the trial court and the Himachal Pradesh High Court on the ground that the 13 year old victim had consented to have sex with the accused Mangaram, the apex court said 'whether there was consent or not is to be ascertained by a careful study of all relevant circumstances'. The apex court further said, 'from the evidence on record it cannot be said that the victim had given consent; there was credible evidence that the victim had offered resistance to prevent the sexual act'. Consent for the purpose of section 375 IPC requires voluntary participation after the exercise of intelligence based on knowledge of the significance and moral quality of the act, the court added.

[*The Times of India*, 26.08. 2000]

74. Extra-judicial confession – basis of conviction in a murder case

One Vinayak Shivaji Rao, a sepoy in the Army, confessed on February 17, 1983 before his superior officers that he had murdered his wife Vimal and signed his confessional statement to that effect. The Army officers informed the police of the statement of the sepoy. The police investigated the case and filed charge sheet. However, the court of sessions acquitted the accused on the ground that other evidence in the case did not corroborate the extra-judicial confession. On appeal the High Court reversed the judgment and sentenced Vinayak to death. It relied upon the crux of the confessional statement and proceeded on the footing that the other details in the statement were not of much relevance and if there was variation in such details, it was not of much consequence. There was no motive on the part of the Army officers to attribute an unlawful statement on the accused, the High Court said. In fact, during investigation, the severed head of the deceased was discovered at the instance of Vinayak.

The Supreme Court upheld the conviction but reduced the sentence to life imprisonment. It also laid down that the court could rest its conclusion on uncorroborated extra-judicial confession particularly when there is no ambiguity in the statement.

[Law Bulletin, SVP National Police Academy, March/April, 1998]

75. Disclosure statement before registration of FIR—not valid as evidence

The police had secret information that some terrorists from Punjab would carry out explosions in some parts of Delhi. On April 6,1993 the police on suspicion nabbed one Monoranjan who disclosed that someone had stockpiled explosives in a particular house. The police searched the house and recovered 2 kg of RDX and a time device. Subsequently, the police charge-sheeted the case (registered after the recovery) against Monoranjan among others. When the case reached the Supreme Court on appeal, the disclosure statement made by Monoranjan was rejected by the court on the ground that it was made before the registration of the case and hence inadmissible as evidence under section 27 of Evidence Act.

The point made in this judgment was that any statement made by an accused and leading to recovery of something of evidentiary value will be valid under section 27 Evidence Act only when the related case is under investigation and not otherwise.

[Monoranjan Singh *vs* State of Delhi, 1998 (1) Crimes 209 (SC)]

76. Governors can okay a minister's prosecution

The Supreme Court has ruled that the Governor of a State can accord sanction for prosecution of a minister for an illegal act even after the council of ministers had refused permission for such prosecution. Allowing an appeal by the M.P. Special Police, the apex court said that if the Governor could not act in his own discretion in such a situation, there would be a complete breakdown of the rule of law as the government may refuse sanction in spite of there being overwhelming materials showing that a *prima facie* case was well made out. The Supreme Court further set aside a High Court order holding that sanction for prosecution of a minister was not a function, which could be exercised by a Governor in his discretion under Article 163 of the Constitution.

[*The Telegraph*, 06. 11. 2004]

77. Judgments cannot be assailed under Article 32: SC

The Supreme Court has said that its judgments cannot be assailed under Article 32 of the Constitution, but a litigant will have remedy against gross miscarriage of justice through 'a curative writ' subject to fulfillment of certain conditions. Disposing a bunch of writ petitions, a bench consisting of Chief Justice SP Barucha, Justices SSM Quadri, VC Banerjee, SN Variava and Shivraj Patil said, 'such petitions can only be filed on limited grounds'.

[*Assam Tribune*, 11. 04. 2002]

78. High Court must show reason for bail order reversal

The Supreme Court has said that the High Courts must show reasons if and when they reverse the order given by trial courts on the bail pleas of the accused persons. Justice Hegde writing for the bench said, "The reasons to be given by the High Court need not be very detailed or elaborate, lest it may cause prejudice to the case of the parties but must be sufficiently indicative of the process of reasoning leading to the passing of the order. The need for delivering a reasoned order is a requirement of law which has to be complied with."

[*Indian Express*, 06. 02. 2004.]

79. Apex Court broadens scope of intervention

The Supreme Court has held that when there has been a gross miscarriage of justice in a criminal case even at the level of a High Court, and at the same time the State fails to prefer an appeal, it would be lawful for a private party to file an appeal before the Supreme Court. "Where a judgment of acquittal by the HC has led to miscarriage of justice, this court cannot refrain from doing its duty and abstain from interfering on the ground that a private party and not the State has invoked the court's jurisdiction", the apex court said upholding the right of appeal against acquittal. "Article 136 is a special jurisdiction. It is residuary power; it is extra ordinary in its amplitude; its limits when it chases injustice is the sky itself," Justices A. Pasayat and D. Raju said in a judgment.

80. SC defines juvenile status

The Supreme Court has ruled that the date of the commission of an offence will determine whether an accused will be entitled to the benefit of the Juvenile Justice Act (JJA). An accused below 18 years is tried under JJA and is entitled to leniency if sentenced.

The SC also held that those being tried as normal criminals for offences committed by them when they were between 16 and 18 years would now be reverted to the juvenile courts if the JJ Act 2000 had come into force by then.

[*The Times of India*, 4.2. 2005]

81. SC on child marriages

Keeping in view the solemnisation of thousands of child marriages every year on the occasion of *Akshay tritiya*, *Ram navami*, *Basant panchami*, etc, the Supreme Court has asked the Collectors and the Superintendents of Police to prevent mass child-marriages. The direction came during a hearing of a PIL seeking stringent action against officials failing to prevent mass child-marriages.

[*The Times of India*, 23. 03.2005]

82. Hospitals must admit emergency cases

A hospital, which refused to attend to a road accident victim for non-payment of Rs 10,000/- as admission fee right at the time of his arrival at the hospital, leading to his death, has been taken to task by a State level Consumer Court. The court reiterated that all 'emergency' patients enjoy the rights of a consumer even before they pay any money to the hospital.

Stressing that human life could not be bartered for money, the Delhi State Consumer Commission president Justice JD Kapoor said: 'Refusal of any hospital or nursing home to admit such a person for treatment on the ground of non-payment of admission fee amounts to deficiency in service, rendering it liable to pay heavy compensation for loss or injury the person suffers'.

[*The Times of India*, 07. 05. 2005]

83. Murder and inherit: SC disqualifies criminal kin

The Supreme Court has ruled that a son, who is sentenced for murdering his father with a motive to acquire his estate, is disqualified to inherit the estate. Even the wife and children of such a person are disentitled to inheritance. The SC quoted a Privy Council decision of 1924 which said, 'A person who is guilty of murder cannot be treated to have any relationship whatsoever with the deceased's estate'.

[*The Times of India*, 12. 5. 2005]

84. Car purchased on car loan

Earlier the system was as follows: If, despite repeated opportunities to repay outstanding car loan instruments, a borrower refused to sign papers returning the vehicle to the finance company, the recovery agents could intimate the local police and seize the vehicle. However, the vehicle should not have been plying on road at the time of taking possession.

New order: The Delhi State Consumer Commission has said that informing the local police is not enough. Recovery agents have to be armed with a civil court's order before taking possession of a car for default in loan repayment.

[*The Times of India*, 27. 10. 2003/30. 03. 2005]

85. Misuse of preventive detention powers an irreparable damage to victim's reputation

The Supreme Court has ruled that the misuse of the power of preventive detention by an authority causes an irreparable damage to the reputation of the victim. Reputation of a person in the society is a facet of the citizen's fundamental right to life and liberty and hence arbitrary use of legal power in ordering such detention is violative of the Constitution.

A bench consisting of Justices Altamas Kabir and Markandey Katju, while quashing on November 12, 2008 a detention order passed under COFEPOSA, built on the general law laid down by a larger Bench in 1994 that the existence of the power to arrest could not itself be a justification for the exercise of that power.

The apex court had ruled in 1994 in Joginder Kumar *vs* State of Uttar Pradesh: "The police officer must be able to justify the arrest apart from showing the power to do so."

The judgment has been hailed by various quarters as pathbreaking. Ashok Arora, a former secretary of the Supreme Court Bar Association, said "the importance of the judgment stems from the fact that in the current scenario, the authorities tend to arrest on frivolous grounds causing an enormous damage even if such persons are released subsequently." The president of the Delhi High Court Bar Association, KC Mittal, welcomed the judgment saying, "Its purpose is not to stop the authorities from arresting suspects. Rather, it is meant to signal to the authorities that they should have firm grounds for making an arrest. They cannot be casual about a person's right to reputation." A former High Court judge Prem Kumar views the ruling as "yet another step in the field of personal liberty".

The judicial pronouncement significantly makes the way clear for arrestees detained on unsure grounds to sue the authorities concerned for causing irretrievable damage to their reputation in public life.

[*The Times of India*, November 16, 2008]

86. No permission required for further investigation by police: SC

The Supreme Court has ruled that police need not seek prior permission of the court for carrying out further investigation in a case but it is a 'must' during re-investigation.

A bench comprising Justices SB Sinha and L Singh Panta, allowing an appeal of the State of Andhra Pradesh in a case relating to charges under section 199/200 IPC, said, "Indisputably, the law does not mandate taking of prior permission from the magistrate for further investigation. Carrying out of a further investigation even after filing of charge-sheet is a statutory right of the police. A distinction also exists between further investigation and re-investigation. Re-investigation without prior permission is forbidden under the law".

The issue came up when the State CID, on orders of its ADG, took over the case of a false claim made by the owner of a timber godown after it was gutted in a fire incident and filed a second charge-sheet against the claimant in addition to the one filed by the local police. The accused had challenged the ADG's order for further investigation of the case on the ground that prior permission of the court was not taken for further investigation.

[*The Sentinel*, December 17, 2007]

In partial modification done on the above ruling, the apex court has now ruled that the police cannot effect radical changes in the crux of a charge-sheet by filing an additional charge-sheet after conducting 'further probe'. This, in effect, means that if the police have made a person an accused in the first charge-sheet, they cannot give him a clean chit while submitting an additional charge-sheet.

[*The Times of India*, April 4, 2009]

87. Gap between expiry and renewal is 'no policy' period

The gap between the points in time of expiry of insurance and its renewal is considered as a 'no policy' period. If an accident takes place during this period, even though the gap is of just a few hours, the insurance company would not be liable to pay compensation to the victim involving the vehicle, said the Supreme Court. In a judgment pronounced in July 2007 by a bench comprising Justices AK Mathur and Dalveer Bhandari, the apex court said that the effectiveness of the insurance policy would start from the time and date specifically incorporated in the policy.

The judgment absolved the National Insurance Corporation of the liability to pay a huge sum. Setting aside a Gauhati High Court order, the apex court said even though the date of renewal was the same, that is July 20, 1994, when the accident occurred at 9 am, there was no valid policy at the time as it was renewed only at 2 pm.

[*The Times of India*, July 13, 2007]

Chapter - III

Departmental Proceedings

Departmental Proceedings are a series of formal actions initiated and taken by the Government (be it the Central Government or a State Government) or a Department concerned under a Government in respect of a government servant's lapses in duties or misconduct. It comprises the followings:

(a) An initial information or report on the alleged lapse or misconduct;

(b) Preliminary enquiry and decision to hold a departmental enquiry;

(c) Issue of charges/statement of allegations (show cause notice);

(d) Written reply of the delinquent;

(e) Appointment of Enquiry Officer (EO);

(f) Holding of enquiry by the EO by way of recording oral, documentary and circumstantial evidences in presence of the delinquent, giving the latter an opportunity to rebut the evidences by cross-examination/re-examination of the prosecution witnesses (PWs);

(g) Submission by the EO of his findings (in the form of a report) to the Disciplinary Authority;

(h) Furnishing of a copy of the EO's findings to the delinquent to afford him an opportunity to represent against the punishment proposed to be inflicted on him;

(i) Consideration of the representation of the delinquent and issuance of final order by the disciplinary authority/competent authority;

(j) Disposal of appeal/review petition, if any, by the Appellate Authority. The term 'appellate authority' also includes the Administrative Tribunal concerned.

Preliminary enquiry

If the initial information or report received by the competent authority[1] does not indicate the existence of enough materials for ordering a formal departmental enquiry (in other words - a departmental proceeding) against a government servant reported against, the said authority may order a preliminary enquiry to find out if the allegations of misconduct of the delinquent were based on facts that could warrant a formal enquiry.

The competent authority should designate an officer by name to make the preliminary enquiry and the designated officer then has to personally conduct the enquiry and submit his report to the authority.

An anonymous petition giving some adverse but vague information against a government servant is ordinarily filed and not acted upon unless there are in it specific instances of misconduct having a bearing on public interest.

Suspension

1. Only the appointing authority/disciplinary authority is competent to order suspension of a government servant. However, as per rules, the authority, to which 'the appointing authority' is subordinate, may also suspend a government servant. Suspension may take place when a disciplinary proceeding is either pending or contemplated against the delinquent or when a case of a criminal offence is under investigation or trial against him.
2. The rationale behind suspension is that the delinquent, if he continues in office, may (a) tamper with documents, (b) intimidate or influence the witnesses, (c) subvert discipline, and (d) cause erosion of public confidence in the government.
3. Suspension, however, is no punishment. It is an administrative act, which is entirely under the discretion of the disciplinary authority. It is resorted to only when there is a report of grave misconduct (criminal or otherwise) on the part of the government servant, - a conduct which is likely to lead to the imposition of a major penalty on him.
4. A government servant under order of suspension has to be granted subsistence allowance (SA) by the disciplinary authority. Refusal

1 The term 'competent authority' is co-terminous with the terms 'disciplinary authority' and 'appointing authority'.

to or delay in sanctioning SA is a violation of the fundamental right of the government servant concerned under Article 21 (right to life and liberty) of the Constitution.

5. A government servant, who is detained in custody, whether on a criminal charge or otherwise, for a period exceeding forty-eight hours, shall be deemed to have been suspended with effect from the date of such detention (arrest) by an order of the appointing authority and shall remain under suspension until further orders.
6. It is the duty of the government servant concerned, who has been arrested for any reason, to intimate the facts and circumstances of his arrest to his official superior promptly.
7. Suspension takes effect from the date of the order. Order of suspension giving retrospective effect is not permissible.
8. Departmental enquiry initiated against a government servant may continue even after he retires from service.
9. It is not permissible for a suspended government servant to accept a private employment or do any business while under suspension without the permission of the competent authority.
10. A government servant under suspension is subject to all the service rules and cannot leave the station without the permission of his official superior. He may, however, make a prayer for change of headquarters for some valid reason.
11. SA granted to a government servant under suspension is ordinarily equivalent to half of the leave salary he is entitled to get if he is on earned leave. If the period of suspension exceeds six months, the authority may increase the SA by a maximum of 50 per cent of the amount of the SA already being drawn. If the departmental enquiry gets prolonged due to dilatory tactics adopted by the government servant, the authority may reduce the increased SA by 50 per cent of the amount initially granted.

Charges and statement of allegations

1. It is only the disciplinary authority, which can issue and communicate the charges and the statement of allegations to the delinquent government servant. A disciplinary authority is the one that has the power to impose the penalties prescribed in the service rules, beginning with a mere reprimand and extending up to dismissal. The following penalties can be imposed on a delinquent government servant for good and sufficient reasons found during an inquiry made under Article 311 (2) of the Constitution.

(a) Censure;

(b) Withholding of annual increments or promotion;

(c) Recovery from pay of an amount equivalent to the pecuniary (monetary) loss suffered by the government owing to the negligence of the government servant;

(d) Reduction in rank/scale of pay/grade;

(e) Compulsory retirement;

(f) Removal from service;

(g) Dismissal from service.

No pension is to be granted to a government servant on his dismissal or removal from service. However, compassionate gratuity may be granted.

When DP is not necessary

Drawal of departmental proceedings is not necessary in the following cases:

(a) Withholding the increments for not passing departmental examinations.

(b) Stopping the government servant at the efficiency bar.

(c) Rejection of the prayer of the government servant for promotion to a higher post or grade after due consideration of his case.

(d) Reversion from an officiating capacity to his permanent post or rank.

(e) Termination of service during or immediately after the probation period.

(f) Compulsory retirement after completion of 25 or 30 years of qualifying service in accordance with Service (Pension) Rules or after attainment of 50 years of age under the relevant Fundamental Rules [2]

[The Supreme Court has ruled that the Government has absolute right to compulsorily retire an employee if his conduct becomes untenable to public interest or obstructs the efficiency of public service.]

---

2 In Assam, it is the Assam Services (Pension) Rules 1969/FR 56 (b).

Integrity

'Integrity of government employees is the foremost consideration in public service.'

The ruling was given by a bench of Justice VN Khare and Justice A Bhan upholding a decision of the UP Government to compulsorily retire an Executive Engineer on the basis of the adverse remarks on his character roll. 'While doing so, the Government was entitled to take into account the service record and the ACRs with emphasis on the later entries.' Dead woods need be removed to maintain efficiency in public service, the Court said.

[*The Telegraph*, 18.03.2002]

Warning

A superior officer may issue to a government servant a written warning, admonition or reprimand if he finds the latter negligent, careless or dilatory in his duties. This is done if the officer does not want to take the formal action of ordering a departmental enquiry after considering the facts and circumstances of the omission or commission on the part of the government servant.

If the circumstances justify, the issuance of such warning or reprimand may be entered in the ACR of the delinquent after observing the principle of natural justice.

Procedures in departmental enquiry

1. The disciplinary authority will frame charges on the basis of the statement of allegations and communicate the same to the delinquent government servant, who will have to submit a written statement in his defence within a specified time limit stating whether he desired to be heard in person.
2. The delinquent will be allowed to inspect and take extracts from the documents on which the charges are based. The authority may refuse such permission if it feels that the documents in question are not relevant or it will be against public interest to allow the delinquent access to them.
3. The disciplinary authority may itself conduct the enquiry or appoint an inquiry officer. The inquiry officer is to be appointed only after the written statement is received.
4. The disciplinary authority will nominate a person to present the case

in support of the charges before the inquiry officer. The delinquent will be allowed to take the assistance of any other government servant of his choice for his defence. He can engage a lawyer for the purpose only if the authority gives a special permission or the presenting officer nominated is himself a lawyer.

5. The inquiry officer will record oral testimony of witnesses and consider the documentary evidences presented from both sides. Cross-examination is allowed.
6. At the conclusion of the enquiry, the inquiring officer will prepare a report recording the findings on each of the charges with reasons therefor.
7. The disciplinary authority, having regard to the findings in the inquiry, may pass appropriate orders as it thinks fit[3] and it shall not be necessary to give the delinquent any opportunity of making a representation on the penalties proposed (vide the 42nd Amendment of the Constitution in 1976).
8. It is mandatory that the delinquent will be communicated the order of the disciplinary authority, furnishing, along with the order, a copy of the inquiry report in the proceedings.

The Supreme Court has, however, laid down the following law in Union of India and Others vs Mohd Ramzan Khan [AIR 1991 SC 471]:

Although on account of the 42nd amendment of the Constitution, it is no longer necessary to issue a notice to the delinquent employee to show cause against the punishment proposed and therefore to furnish a copy of the inquiry officer's report along with the notice to make representation (if desired) against the penalty, whenever the inquiry officer is other than the disciplinary authority, the delinquent employee is entitled to a copy of the report to enable him to make a representation to the authority. Non-furnishing of the same is a violation of the rules of natural justice. The delinquent employee should have the benefit of the report of the inquiry officer before the disciplinary authority records its findings on the charges leveled against him.

Important points emerging from various decisions in D.P.s

1. There is nothing called honourable acquittal in CrPC It appears only in departmental enquiries.

3 In Assam, it is as per Rule 9 (10) of the Assam Services (Discipline and Appeal) Rules 1964.

2. On acquittal of a suspended government from a criminal case, he will be entitled to full pay for the period of suspension.
3. Where an acquittal is on technical grounds, the State has the right to refuse full pay and allowances for the period of suspension.
4. When a government servant is dismissed from service, the earlier order of suspension automatically comes to an end. If the dismissal order is later set aside, it does not revive the order of suspension.
5. A written warning amounts to censure, as it will affect the career of the government servant if put on record. Such an order is appealable.
6. A casual labourer is not a holder of a post.
7. Officiating and temporary government servants are entitled to the protection of Article 311.
8. Discharge of a probationer cannot be questioned except on the basis of *malafides* in the making of the order.
9. A preliminary enquiry to determine whether a *prima facie* case exists for holding a departmental enquiry would not attract Article 311.
10. Every government has the inherent executive power to create and abolish a post in the interest of public service.
11. When the President or a Governor issues a dismissal order on a government servant in the interest of security of the State under Article 311 (2) (c) of the Constitution, no court can intervene on the ground of denial of opportunity of an enquiry to him.
12. Reasonable opportunity to a delinquent government servant means the opportunity
    (a) to deny his guilt and establish his innocence. This he may do by making a defence statement, cross-examining the prosecution witnesses and producing defence witnesses and documents.
    (b) to make a representation against a proposed penalty.
13. In a departmental enquiry, it is enough if communications are sent to the delinquent by Registered Post A/D. If the delinquent refuses service, it will be at his risk.
14. The disciplinary authority cannot base its decision on any evidence supposedly tendered by a witness without the latter being examined orally in the departmental enquiry. This is against the rules of natural justice.

15. The right to cross-examine a witness is a most valuable right.
16. If punishment is proposed, among other things, on the basis of previous records, the said things should be disclosed in the initial show cause notice itself.
17. The delinquent is entitled to have beforehand the copies of all documents to be cited in the inquiry in order to be able to cross-examine PWs during oral examination.
18. If the delinquent under suspension is short of funds owing to non-payment of SA and unable to attend the inquiry, *ex-parte* proceedings are vitiated.
19. In a case of grave nature when a criminal case has been instituted and departmental proceedings are also initiated on the same set of facts, it is advisable for the disciplinary authority to await the decision of the trial court before a final order is passed in the proceedings. The accused government servant in such a case may take a plea that his defence in the criminal case got prejudiced if the DP is carried forward.
20. The power to take disciplinary action is vested in the disciplinary authority and not the court.
21. Departmental action is possible on the variant of the charges of corruption, which had earlier led to acquittal by a court of law.
22. Departmental Proceedings are quasi-judicial in nature.
23. Once a decision is arrived at honestly by a competent authority, its successor in office, after the decision has been acted upon, cannot reconsider the matter to take a totally different decision.
24. To act judicially in an administrative matter means to act justly and fairly and not arbitrarily and capriciously.
25. The aim of the rules of natural justice is to secure justice and prevent miscarriage of justice.
26. A 'speaking order' giving out the salient features of the case and the reasons for arriving at a decision must always be recorded by an authority, whether disciplinary or appellate, when it disposes of a case. Thc 'speaking order' discloses the reasoning behind the decision.
27. Charges must be specific and to the point regarding the date, place or person, etc. Vague charges make it impossible for the delinquent to defend himself as he is left to guess about the material particulars on which the charges are sought to be established.

28. Order of punishment issued only on the basis of ambiguous admission of guilt and without any formal enquiry suffers from fatal infirmity and should be avoided. Issue of such an order on the basis of admission will not be in order.
29. Evidence on which the prosecution relies must be made available to the delinquent as per the rules of natural justice.
30. In cases where evidence is of circumstantial nature, the circumstances should, in the first place, be fully established. The facts so established should be consistent with the hypothesis (supposition) of the guilt of the accused. The chain of evidence should be so complete as not to leave a reasonable ground for a conclusion consistent with the innocence of the accused. It must be such that, within all human probability, the act must have been done by the accused.
31. Suspicion can never take the place of proof.
32. Disciplinary authority is free to agree or disagree, wholly or partly, with the findings of the inquiring officer since the latter works as a delegate of the former.
33. The inquiry officer must choose the venue of the inquiry on his own accord.
34. If the delinquent government servant wants to produce defence witness, every facility in this regard should be given to him.
35. An order is an order when it is expressed in the name of the appropriate authority and communicated to the person intended to be affected.
36. Compulsory retirement is not a penal action. Government has the absolute right to retire a government servant if it is in public interest to do so.
37. Transfer to a post carrying the same scale of pay and rank but not the same status does not amount to reduction in rank.
38. Removal of the name from a select list for promotion does not amount to reduction in rank.
39. A mere suspicion of bias is not sufficient. There must be a reasonable likelihood of bias.
40. An administrative action cannot override a statutory rule.
41. A court cannot sit in judgement over the process of decision-making by a disciplinary authority where the accused has been

given prior opportunity to defend himself.

42. It is not the function of a court of law to examine.
    (i) whether the material on record should be taken as sufficient by an authority to hold the accused guilty.
    (ii) whether the punishment was too severe.
43. Circumstances where the court of law may interfere in departmental proceedings are:
    (i) where the rules of natural justice are violated.
    (ii) where the statutory rules prescribing the mode of enquiry are offended.
    (iii) where considerations extraneous to the evidence in or merits of the case are taken into account.
    (iv) where the conclusion on the very face of it is so wholly arbitrary or capricious that no reasonable person could come to such a conclusion.
44. If it is proved that there is no evidence to support the conclusion of the disciplinary authority/appellate authority, a writ of *certiorari* may issue under Article 226 of the Constitution.
45. Once resignation has been accepted, it is no longer possible for a public servant to withdraw it, even if acceptance of the resignation has not been communicated to him.
46. Termination of service by an order passed by the government does not take effect till the order is actually communicated to the government servant.
47. Once the previous bad record is condoned, it cannot be allowed to influence judgement for the purpose of compulsory retirement.

Appellate authority/Administrative Tribunal

Departmental service rules indicate the appointing authority/disciplinary authority and the appellate authority for different categories of government servants in a department. A government servant aggrieved by the orders of his disciplinary authority in respect of his service matters can prefer an appeal to the designated appellate authority.

After an aggrieved government servant had exhausted all the levels of his departmental hierarchy, he may prefer an appeal to the Administrative Tribunal concerned for redress. This he must do within a time limit prescribed in the relevant legislation relating to the tribunal.

An administrative tribunal normally does not have jurisdiction to entertain an appeal against an order of punishment passed by a disciplinary authority/government under Article 311 (2) provisos (a), (b) and (c) of the Constitution. These provisos relate to:

(i) an order passed after criminal conviction of the government servant in a court of law.

(ii) an order passed after declaring that it was not reasonably practicable to hold an enquiry.

(iii) an order passed by the President of India or the Governor of the State concerned affirming that an enquiry could not be held in that regard in the interest of the security of the state.

An order passed by an administrative tribunal is final so far as departmental remedies are concerned. Such a tribunal is always vested with the powers of a civil court in respect of enforcing attendance of any person, requiring production of documents, requisitioning public records and issuing commission for examining witnesses and documents.

Chapter - IV

Gender Violence:
Focus, Manifestation and Strategy

The problem

Violence is the wrongful application of force by a strong person upon a weak person. It could be perpetrated to achieve certain objectives, which may even include an urge to take revenge. The ultimate purpose of violence is the domination of the weak (victim) by the strong (perpetrator). Gender violence is but a manifestation of this phenomenon that takes a variety of forms, following essentially from a desire to give expression to a superior male ego. It is an act of aggression by an economically or physically or otherwise stronger male upon a person of the weaker sex. In its modern definition, it includes, among other things, physical acts of abuse and neglect, verbal abuse and denial of proper food and other necessities of life[1]. Such violence is, in most cases, sadistic and in violation of all civilized norms of life. The growth of human civilization from the savage and later barbaric stage has seen a great many upheavals and the standard by which we can judge the level of a civilization is the way its women are treated. That we have not yet reached the desired level of civilization is apparent from a UN Report (1980) that says as follows:

"Women constitute half of world's population, perform two thirds of its work hours, receive one tenth of world's income and less than one hundredth of its property."

Here deprivation caused to women is the main theme. This 'deprivation' is not without violence or threat of violence. Thus, it is forced upon the womenfolk.

---

1 Malavika Karlekar—Domestic Violence, Oxford Handbook of Indian Sociology (p. 308).

Elsewhere, it has been said: "Whatever women do, they must do twice as well as men to be thought half as good." (*Charlotte Whitton*) In reality, this is the situational placement of women.

Based on these findings, it is well established that women as a class are in a weak position *vis-à-vis* their male counterparts. However, a social system that encourages the strong to trample upon the rights of the weak can never be, by any consideration, a civilized way of life and it therefore becomes extremely reprehensible when the male folk-- being physically stronger than women-- resort to physical violence to bring the latter to submit themselves before them.

Forms of Gender Violence

Gender violence takes multifarious forms, like molestation, eve teasing[2], sexual harassment at workplace, kidnapping, rape, forced labour, forced prostitution, forced marriage, foeticide, infanticide, sati, dowry death, honour killing, witch-hunting[3] domestic violence, and so on. Among all the crimes against women, rape and domestic violence constitute 5% of the total burden on women.[4] Each of these offences mentioned above is punishable under the law and 'cognizable'[5] to the police in India for initiating action against the perpetrators of the crimes. However, the saddest part of the Indian situation is that despite there being stringent provisions of law against these offences, they are continuously on the rise. Another aspect of the matter is that many of the incidents relating to these crimes are not even reported by the victim or her family for fear of 'shame' and even the ones that are reported do not receive proper attention, especially due to sluggishness of the police machinery and the judicial system. Age-old prejudices based on superstitions and systematic infliction of 'dishonour' on women-- which have some degree of religious sanction in India-- are a great deal responsible for the perpetuation of many of the heinous crimes committed against them.

---

2 It can be termed as sexual harassment at public place

3 Witch-hunting is widely prevalent among certain tribes in Assam, Jharkhand, Chattisgarh, M.P. and some other States in central India.

4 World Development Report (1993)

5 Where the police has the legal power to investigate the incident and arrest the offender without warrant.

Women are generally discriminated against since before their birth and it continues life long. A female foetus is aborted because parents are keen to have a son instead of a daughter, maybe for the prospect of the son looking after them at a later stage or maybe to avoid paying dowry at the time of the daughter's marriage. Religious beliefs further enhance the desire to have a son rather than a daughter. The cruel practice of female infanticide is resorted to precisely for the same reasons.

The practice of sati, though abolished by the then British government in 1829, had to be banned once again by an Act of Parliament in 1987 when a peculiarly barbaric Indian mindset manifested itself in the Deorala incident in which a young widow was burnt alive following her husband's natural death. Killing or abetting suicide of brides for dowry is as widespread even now as it was over the years. Law till now has not been able to catch up with the enormity of the problem and thus dowry deaths remain a common phenomenon in India without any sign of abating.

Caste differences and superstitious beliefs, on the other hand, are at the root of 'honour killing' of young women who dare to break the taboos of caste and other prejudices to go for marriage with someone who is supposedly from a lower caste or a different religion.[6] So-called minor offences like outrage of modesty, eve-teasing, sexual harassment at workplace, etc. are an every day affair, which women have to face day in and day out in public transport, at the roads or at office or factory or in the course of other business. Needless to say that there is always an implied threat of the probable use of violence against the victim even in these smaller offences. Female genital mutilation is another savage crime some communities indulge in owing to a sickening superstition they suffer from.

Domestic violence, which is but a form of gender violence--a species in the genus -- has, of late, been growing very rapidly all over the country, so much so that the Central Government had to bring in a legislation in 2005 to meet the growing menace. The worst form of gender-based crime is, however, the rape of a woman or a girl child, which causes a total physical and mental trauma in her.

Rape is followed these days by murder of the victim (by the rapist himself) in a number of cases. This is done by the rapist to eliminate

6 The incidence of 'honour-killing' in Pakistan is even higher than that in India.

the possibility of the victim identifying him during investigation later and telling the police about his part in the crime. In some cases, even infants or kids do not escape the brutal assault of a rapist.

Forced labour, marriage and prostitution, where the use of force on the hapless victim is the basic element of the crime, are also rampant, especially in the Indian sub-continent and other South Asian countries. The tragedy of such happenings is that a sensitive victim sometimes chooses the escapist way of inflicting death on herself rather than seeking to bring the culprit to justice. And even in those cases where a brave woman tries to break out of this problematic situation, the social environment is such that it is not possible for her to achieve a favourable result.

Working women, at the same time, are not immune to aggression of their male colleagues who seek sexual favours from them right at their workplaces (or at some other place of the latter's choice). The male psychology pervading such an event is just the same as that in other types of violent crimes against women. Everywhere the perpetrator of violence takes advantage of the disadvantageous position of the weaker sex owing particularly to the latter's economic dependence and lesser physical strength as well as an unfavourable social climate.

The above forms of gender violence are not exhaustive. There are many subtle forms in which most of the gender crimes are committed. All forms of crimes against women (as described above) are but a deeply rooted social malaise, many of which owe their origin to a number of abominable pitfalls in our social mores. These social mores shaped up over centuries, thanks to superstitious beliefs and prejudices that got exacerbated, in many cases, by misinterpretations of the ancient scriptures. Conservativeness that developed during and after the foreign invasions in the middle age of Indian history also contributed a great deal to the society's attitude to women. They were looked upon as expendable. The idea of male domination that originated from some of our ancient literatures influenced the thinking of generations of Indians, many of whom succumbed to the influence of wrong ideas. That's how a male perpetrating inhuman atrocity on a woman feels no compunction about his deeds; instead he boasts about it as an expression of his masculine power and feels satisfied about it. The society at large, being imbued with the same value system, also remains more or less indifferent to such brutal behaviour by the menfolk on women.

The conspiratorial negligence on the part of the sons and daughters of helpless widows for their mothers and the indifference of the society and the legal system (including the laws of inheritance) towards them are nothing but a passive crime against such women. The hundreds of widows, who are thrown to their fate at, among other places, Brindaban and Varanasi, are living examples of the societal attitude towards old and infirm women. The added disadvantage they suffer from is that most of them are totally illiterate and cannot even communicate except in the language or dialect of their own. For them, these 'holy places' they are placed at are like a foreign land. Some of these widows are pushed to these places at a relatively young age and are exploited sexually and treated invariably harshly all along. The widows placed at these religious places survive for years and even decades without even the modicum of health care because they are unable to die straight away. This undignified existence of widows[7] is a direct violation of their right to live with dignity at its minimum.

Who is responsible for the hellish situation in which a great number of women in India find themselves but about which the males do not even have to bother? It is the depraved value system that we inherited and care to sustain. Here it is to be noted that though crimes against women do exist in different degrees all over the world, those that are committed in India are much graver in intensity. The practice of marrying out the girl child to older men,[8] the treatment of widows in the way it is done, religious prostitution in temples,[9] etc. are singularly Indian in nature. Shall all these go on for all time? The following Table presents a picture of the pattern in which gender crimes have been occurring in India:

---

7 Jnanpith award winner Ms Mamoni Raisom Goswami of Assam, in her articles in the print media, had drawn attention of all right-thinking people to this gross violation of human rights of countless number of widows at religious places like Brindaban. This is nothing but an intense form of violence permeated on women with some amount of religious sanction. The victims virtually starve, remain ill clad and suffer indignities for a whole lifetime that spans over decades. By any standard, this is a willful breach by the families concerned and the society at large of the suffering widows' right to life with dignity under Article 21 of the Constitution.

8 This practice is hugely prevalent among both Hindus and Muslims in India.

9 For example, the Devadasi system in Orissa and Andhra Pradesh.

Table I

Registered crime figures

Year	Rape	Kidnapping/ Abduction	Dowry Death	Dowry	Cruelty by husband/ relatives	Child Marriage
2002	16,373	14,506	6,822	2,816	49,237	113
2003	15,847	13,296	6,208	2,684	50,703	63
2004	18,233	15,578	7,026	3,592	58,121	93
2005	18,359	15,750	6,787	3,204	58,319	122
2006	19,348	17,414	7,618	4,504	63,128	
2007	20,737	20,416	8,093	5,623	75,930	
2008	21,467	22,939	8,172	5,555	81,344	
2009	21,397	25,741	8,383	5,650	89,546	
2010	22,172	29,795	8,391	5,182	94,041	

Apart from the above, crimes of a slightly lesser intensity – like molestation, sexual harassment at workplace, immoral trafficking, indecent representation of women, etc. are also on the increase.

[Source: National Crime Records Bureau, New Delhi.]

The way violence against women is handled

The figures above relate to those incidents that have been reported to the police and the courts and are therefore the official crime statistics. What is important here is that in each category of the crimes, there are innumerable incidents, which have never been reported due to the reluctance or inability of the victims (or their families) to file an FIR or a complaint. Instead, in many cases, they choose to take their own lives out of a sense of 'shame' or frustration. Many a time the police refuse to record the FIR for their own reasons, like, for example their obsession with the area jurisdiction,[10] fear of the crime figures in the police station going up, inability to investigate owing to lack of man-power, insensitivity to gender crimes, etc. And even in the recorded cases, justice is a far cry, given the inefficiency and corrupt practices in the working of the police and the slow 'legalistic' approach of the

10 This is in spite of the Supreme Court ruling that registration of an FIR filed in any police station in the country in respect of a cognizable offence is obligatory regardless of its place of occurrence.

judiciary to the crimes. These phenomena are a result of the lack of training and sensitivity of the officials who are supposed to deal with them. It is our experience that in the trials of such criminal cases, the quest is not for the criminal or the actual crime that happened but to find out lacunae in investigation or statements of witnesses so that the perpetrator of the crime could be let off. The theory quoted to justify this approach is that a hundred guilty persons may go unpunished but even one innocent person should not suffer. The Priyadarshini Mattoo case and the Jessica Lal case are shining examples of what happens.[11] Such an approach only emboldens the offender to further commit similar crimes.

Table II

Penal laws in India on crimes against women

	Offence
Indian Panal Code Law	Kidnapping and abduction, Eve-teasing, Outrage of modesty, Rape, Dowry Death, Forced marriage, Murder, etc.
Commission of Sati (Prevention) Act 1987	Offences relating to Sati
Immoral Traffic (Prevention) Act, 1956	Trafficking in women (for prostitution)
Ruling of the Supreme Court in Vishaka *vs* State of Rajasthan, 1997	Sexual Harassment At Workplace (A legislation on this is in process now.)
The Protection of Women from Domestic Violence Act, 2005	A civil law enumerating the rights of women and enforcement thereof. Domestic Violence.
The Dowry (Prohibition) Act, 1961	Giving and receiving of dowry.
The Indecent Representation of Women (Prevention) Act, 1986	As the title implies;

Table contd...

11 In both the cases, the trial court had let off the accused concerned for "lack of evidence" but on the basis of the same set of evidence, the Delhi High Court convicted and sentenced them to death and life imprisonment respectively. Appreciation of evidence should be thoughtful if justice is to be rendered, more so in crimes against women.

The Pre-Natal Diagnostic Techniques (Regulation and Prevention of Misuse) Act, 1994	Female foeticide.
The Medical Termination Of Pregnancy Act, 1971	Causing of abortion.
The Prevention of Child Marriage Act 2006	As the title implies (The present law has travelled a long way from its earlier avatar as "The Child Marriage (Restraint) Act 1929]

The laws mentioned above are, by and large, comprehensive and are in place. However, they are not having a strongly deterrent impact on the incidence of various types of crimes against women. Thus, there is an increasing trend in the incidence of almost all the said crimes creating doubts about the efficacy of the related laws. The problem apparently lies in the implementation of the laws by the government and the judiciary. One of the reasons for the failure of justice for the victims is the lack of sensitivity of the investigating agencies, the prosecutors and the judiciary to the crimes against women. To reverse the present trend would therefore require proper sensitisation of all concerned.

Historical background of the status of women in India

Swami Vivekananda (1863-1901) had made a very important observation:

"That country and that nation which do not respect women have never become great nor will ever be in future"

In ancient India, in the age of *Rig Veda*, the patriarchal society did not deny their women the right to participate in public life and to education. The then laws of marriage and the rules pertaining to sexual morality give us an insight into the extent of liberty enjoyed by women. They were allowed the freedom to choose their partners in life[12] and in running the household. Women's property rights were also recognised to a considerable extent. With reference to this, Manu the law-giver had later said, 'gods are pleased with those households where women are held in honour'. In this age, the husband and the wife came to be known as *Dampati* and they had a relation of

12 The practice was known as '*Swambara*'.

reciprocity. The woman had full autonomy in her sphere of activity. Women even joined community deliberations and sacrificial rites[13] including the study of the *Vedas*. They also had a considerable role in agriculture, weaving of clothes and other economic activities. All these enhanced their position in the general scheme of things. The term '*Patni*' was applied to the wife in the *Brahmanas*[14], a fact that indicates her equal share in socio-religious side of her husband's life. At the time of the *Upanishads*, there have been references to high intellectual attainments of women scholars. Gargi, Maitreyi and many other gifted ladies adorned the educational field those days. Obviously, violence on women those days was minimal if at all it was there.

However, the status of women did not remain constant. Women had to discontinue their intellectual pursuits. Manu, in contradiction to his earlier position, declared, "Let the husband employ his wife in the collection and expenditure of wealth, in keeping everything clean in the fulfillment of religious duties, in preparation of his food, and in looking after the household utensils". This dictum, in effect, called for enslavement of women for service to the men folk. Thus came the beginning of an inferior status for women. They lost their say in matters that concerned their own life. This situation, therefore, opened up a pathway to violence against them.

In later years, women were reduced to the status of '*sudra*'[15]. The deterioration started from 300 BC onwards. They came to be regarded as '*minors*' in the eye of law; as a girl, a woman had to be under the tutelage of her parents; as a wife, of her husband, and as a widow, of her sons. In the *Anusasana Parva* of the *Mahabharata*, on being queried by Yudhisthira, Bhisma was reported to have said, "Woman always stands in need of protection by men." The Buddhist *Jataka* stories give an adverse projection of female character and created a

13 *Yagnas* – an important religious ritual of the *Aryans*.

14 Hindu religious literature

15 The members of the lowest caste that was denied most of the human rights and dealt with very cruelly.

negative image for women. The institutions of *Ganika, Devadasi*, etc were created for engaging women in prostitution for the benefit of the so-called upper classes, including priests. Manu, in his treatise, had laid down very harsh penalties for women even for small offences that might be committed by them. The practice of *sati* gained ground as far back as 400 BC Thus even the most fundamental human right---the right to life and dignity—tended to be denied to women.

All these circumstances cumulatively created a plausible ground for ill-treatment of women by men for their lust and to satisfy their feeling of superiority. The perceptions thus created persisted throughout the Indian history. Varahamihira,[16] however, disapproved of the ideas propagated by so many of the religious authorities and said, "I am convinced that those who disregard the qualities of women and talk about their shortcomings must themselves be bad men; such talk by them is not inspired by bona fide motive."

Women's status and position got further eroded during the medieval period. The fear psychosis emanating from a sense of insecurity for the girl child and women during the Muslim rule led to the popularity of practices like child marriage, *sati*, *jauhar,*[17] etc. Gradually, society came to accept the proposition that the life of a woman was disposable in a violent way. She thus fell victim to the tyranny of thoughtless men whose physical prowess, bodily vigour and muscular strength reduced her to a permanently subordinate position with men having the power of life and death on her. Consequently, women being maltreated, underfed and overworked became the order of the day. They were now expected to accept all these outrages silently and without protest. A clear male bias came to be established in the system. All humanitarian considerations were thrown to winds.

The concept of daughters being *paraya dhan* (somebody else's property) had also added to the social tolerance of a discriminatory approach to women as unequal to the male child in India.

---

16 Scholar living in the court of Guptas.

17 Collective suicide by Rajput women in the face of invasion by a Muslim monarch.

Domestic Violence

The problem of domestic violence is a worldwide phenomenon. It has a very ugly shape in this country. It is the inevitable result of gender inequality and the in-built bias against women in the society. It involves mental, physical, sexual and economic abuse of a woman by a man in the family itself.[18] It is the single biggest crime that, unlike other criminal offences, affects the largest number of victims. What is more traumatising to a woman is the fact that after her marriage, she enters the family set-up completely as a stranger and is hardly acquainted with the power equations in the family. Thus, she cannot immediately develop the required 'personhood' to be able to resist the violence that confronts her on some pretext or the other.

Domestic violence is a crime that exists in the so-called civilised society. It is, in most cases, suffered silently. The impact of this crime is very subtle and its redress is very difficult to achieve. It impacts negatively the healthy growth of a family. Directly or indirectly, it takes the form of child abuse, because a child can never be happy when it sees its mother being abused and the future consequence could be that the child would turn to alcohol or substance abuse or some form of crime, which is most likely to be violent. Any law, however thoughtfully planned, is not adequate to reach out the victim to the full. Any judgment regarding an incident of domestic violence is likely to make an error or two, since independent evidence is difficult to get in such matters. Besides, the legal processes involve a lot of delay to arrive at a decisive stage and that is fatal for the cause of justice in cases of domestic violence. This indeed is the prime reason why many a victim of this type of violence feels shy of taking recourse to law. Then there is the problem of economic dependence on the offender himself that dissuades her from asking for redress. For a mother, the custody of minor children is also a predominant consideration before she could step forward for justice. The expenses for litigation cannot also be borne by a hapless woman because, in such cases, the offender husband holds up even her *stridhan* [19] leaving her as a pauper. The legal aid envisaged in the Legal Services Authorities

18 Section 3, The Protection of Woman from Domestic Violence Act, 2005.

19 Money or valuables that a woman receives at the time of her marriage. In the eye of law, she is the exclusive owner of this property.

Act 1987 as per Article 39A of the Constitution[20] still remains a mirage for an illiterate woman, who neither has the knowledge about the availability of the facility nor has the access to people in charge of it at a given place. This is the reality of life in India.

Rather than going by theories, the real reasons behind wife bashing or domestic violence as found from police files are as follows:

1. Demand for dowry
2. Alcoholism/drug addiction
3. Inherited disposition from father or someone in the family
4. Male superiority complex/intolerance
5. Influence of social environment/influence of family members
6. Unemployment or other economic problems
7. Jealousy, frustration and the like (negative emotions)
8. Lack of education and absence of 'values'
9. Provocation by the victim herself
10. Infidelity, real or suspected
11. Miscellaneous causes

However, all the above are 'acquired' behaviour that originates from a faulty value system. Case studies reflect a picture of widespread prevalence of domestic violence all over the world, no matter the level of culture or literacy the country concerned possesses. Elizabeth Rod-Grange, a Swiss sociologist and activist associated with a women's rights group says: "It is not a question of democracy, education, freedom or civic sense. Which is why the statistics for wife beating are about the same in the developed and the developing world. It is fallacious to think that there is a link between democracy, prosperity, education levels and domestic violence."

There are instances of high-level Bank executives, professors, lawyers and even judges ill-treating their wives even in countries like

20 Inserted by the Constitution (Forty-second Amendment) Act, 1976; it reads: *Equal justice and free legal aid*—The State shall secure that the operation of the legal system promotes justice, on the basis of equal opportunity, and shall, in particular, provide free legal aid, by suitable legislation or schemes or in any other way, to ensure that opportunities for securing justice are not denied to any citizen by reason of economic or other disabilities.

Switzerland, Britain, France and other countries of the 'civilized' West. The story of Julia Rios, a Brazilian born micro-biologist married to a Swiss architect is revealing: she wrote a book[21] in the year 2000 in which she described 'the savage beatings, repeated marital rape, sequestration and financial deprivation' that she suffered in the hands of her husband. She said that the police, the lawmakers and the judges very often display a strong bias against a battered woman. A judge in her case had ruled that her injuries were self-inflicted. Violent partners have 'a hunger for power' over women, she added.

Husbands practicing violence on their wives show an earlier sign of being extremely possessive and jealous, to the extent of resorting to spying on the latter by eavesdropping and other means. Their expression of love disguises their internal jealousy. The society's attitude to domestic violence, on the other hand, is guided by a false assumption that violence between spouses or live-in partners is a private family affair and should not be interfered with by outsiders. Whether it is the police or a neighbour or a colleague, everyone is wary of breaking into a private area, which is considered sacrosanct. Thus help does not come to a battered woman when she needs it most. Another aspect of violence indoors is that when it comes out in the open, there is a 'public washing of dirty linen' to the embarrassment of all. Significantly, it is a scourge from which one out of every five women in the world suffers.

Domestic violence is not confined to the beating of a wife by her husband. The story of a French woman of Algerian descent, Amina, who lives in a Paris suburb, is tellingly illustrative. She had a cut lip, huge bruises around right eye and lived in a shelter-home. She said that there was unimaginable violence in North African immigrant ghettos. "Our fathers, brothers, husbands and boyfriends, all beat us", she said. Many women continue to love their tormentors and therefore are hesitant to accuse them despite being sufferers.

A glimpse of domestic violence abroad

- *12.6% of Swiss women (or more than one in eight) suffer physical violence while 11.6% (or one in nine) suffer sexual violence. As many as 40.3% are affected by psychological violence. On the whole, 20% of Swiss women suffer from domestic violence.*

21 Le Piege (The Trap).

- *In France, one in every three women suffers violence in her lifetime. Six women die each month in the hands of persons who profess that they love them.*
- *In Spain, there are 30,000 complaints of domestic violence every year. The annual death toll of women in the hands of abusive husbands or lovers is a hundred on the average.*
- *In the UK, one woman is killed by her partner every three days and one in four suffers domestic violence.*

[Source: Criminal Investigation Department Review, CB, Tamil Nadu, August 2004]

One aspect of the statistics about the violence on women is that they contain information mainly about urban areas even in western countries. The state of affairs in the countryside in all countries must be grimmer.

The Indian scenario

As the figures in Table I shows, there is a steeply rising trend in the incidence of domestic violence and dowry deaths in India. Here one must say that even if the figures remain constant or go down slowly, it is still bad enough and should put the country's polity to shame. The Protection of Women from Domestic Violence Act, 2005, which is a comprehensive law on this subject and has been officially notified into effect wef October 26, 2006, addresses the core problems of domestic violence in their entirety. There are high expectations from the legislation now. However, the question is how far the law will succeed in giving true redress to the suffering victims.

It is several years now since the issuance of the notification that gave effect to the above law but the state governments are yet to take the requisite actions for setting up *shelter homes* and *counselling centers* and appoint *protection officers* in each district as per the requirements of the Act. It is to be understood that token things done for the above purpose simply won't do. People in charge of such an effort will have to be trained professionals with a humane attitude. Adequate funds must also be allotted for the purpose and there should be independent watchdog bodies to make sure that officials concerned do not eat the same away by corrupt means. Non-Governmental Organisations (NGOs) as provided for in the POWFDV Act have a very important role to play in this regard but they themselves should be under a system of public audit so that graft does not make a room for itself.

Tens of hundreds of NGOs in India have been in existence in paper only without actually contributing anything in substance because funds provided to them are both misused and misappropriated and the office bearers have no accountability. It is also our experience that the office bearers of NGOs are not very clear in many cases as to how they are expected to address the problems they come across.

Strategy to combat domestic violence – an outline

The nodal state government department -- in most cases it is the social welfare department-- should be cleansed even as the job of implementing the law is entrusted to it.

There should be total transparency in the steps taken to implement the law.

NGOs, apart from being service providers,[22] should organise massive awareness and legal literacy programmes to enlighten both men and women about the rights of women under international and national laws and conventions. Men should also be made to participate in these programmes as much as women.

A strong campaign should be initiated to sensitise the police, the lawyers, the judges, the executives, the doctors, the people in all other major professions and, most importantly, the common people all over in the matter of crimes against women in general and domestic violence in particular.

Criminal cases relating to the above should be investigated and tried in a time bound manner. Police officers, medical officers working in the field of Forensic Medicine, public prosecutors and judges should voluntarily take upon themselves the task of ensuring speedy justice in such cases. This they can do by performing their respective roles with a sense of urgency and dedication.

The Media, both electronic and print, should take an active role in highlighting acts of domestic violence and other offences against women (and the girl child) so that the offenders may not only come to suffer penal sentences under the relevant laws but also be ostracised by the society to give an expression to its sense of outrage at such incidents. A convention of zero tolerance to crimes against women should be developed in the social arena. Thus, such offenders would come to realize that crime does not pay and it is not worthwhile to commit one.

---

22 Section 10, POWFDV Act 2005

Protection Officers under section 9 of the POWFDV Act should be given the wherewithal to perform the job envisaged for them in the Act. They will be the supporting pillars for the successful implementation of the Act. If they fail at the grassroots level, the law is bound to fail.

There should be a law to effectively regulate the activities of NGOs without affecting in any way their autonomy and freedom of action.

There ought to be a nationwide uniform system or protocol for medical examination of the victims of gender violence—be it rape or other forms of physical violence—to ensure an objective identification of the nature and causes of such violence for eventual punishment of the offenders. Doctors should have specialised training in the intricate procedures of Forensic Medicine so that violence of any nature on women could be accurately reported upon. This will go a long way to bring perpetrators of violence to justice by significantly raising the rate of conviction in crimes against women.[23]

Last but not the least is the necessity to achieve empowerment of women in social, economical, political and educational fields – as also in health care and nutrition – so that a system of perfect gender equality could be effected in the society in not so distant a future.[24] This is the key to stopping of violence against women. Given the age-old and deep-rooted attitude of discrimination towards women, it will, however, take a lot of time and sustained effort to achieve success in empowering women to the desired level. There will be many hurdles in the process. Social duplicity in blocking the progress of women in the various fields will, therefore, have to be overcome with determination. The insincere approach of the polity in giving women the long awaited reservation of one third of the seats in Parliament and state legislatures is a classic example of the struggle ahead.

Bottom-line

23 The Indian Medical Association has recently undertaken to reform this aspect of the justice delivery system. The Sentinel, March 26, 2007.

24 The UN General Assembly had set the goals of gender equality and women's empowerment to be achieved by member countries by 2015, but a survey conducted by the World Economic Forum in 2006 in this respect placed India in the 53rd position out of 58 countries.

In the road to the destination mentioned above, women themselves have to develop an attitude of self-help and hard work. It has to be remembered that nobody is going to offer women their appropriate place and dues just for mere asking. It has to be acquired by a sustained struggle for emancipation.

Chapter - V

Trafficking in Women and Children

What is Trafficking?

Trafficking in women and children is a common phenomenon all over the world. As the process of globalization is currently under way involving almost all the countries of the world in greater or lesser degree, human trafficking has taken new forms and routes and been exploiting new sources. But before we proceed with the subject, we must know what precisely 'human trafficking' means in the present context. The UN Convention on the Suppression of the Traffic in Persons and the Exploitation of the Prostitution of Others 1949, as amended in 1994, defines trafficking as

"*the illicit and clandestine movement of persons across national and international borders, largely from developing countries and some countries with economies in transition, with the end goal of forcing women and girl children into sexually or economically oppressive and exploitative situations for the profit of recruiters, traffickers, and crime syndicates, as well as other illegal activities related to trafficking, such as forced domestic labour, false marriages, clandestine employment and false adoption.*"

Human cargo

Traffickers target the powerless members of the under-developed society – the poor and illiterate women and children – to make profit out of their poverty, ignorance and misery. Needless to say that the poorest and most illiterate among women and children are the worst sufferers. They are exported in bondage to rich countries for overt and covert prostitution and forced labour. The victims are ordinarily from the third world countries, that is, the under-developed countries where the level of incomes, employment and economic development is very low. The aim of the traffickers is to exploit the victims both sexually and economically. The traffickers are a form of 'crime syndicate' looking for and encashing in a fertile ground. Thus Asian countries like India, Pakistan, Bangladesh, Sri Lanka, Nepal, the Philippines and Vietnam, among others, have a flourishing under-cover trade in the trafficking of women and the girl child and are a perennial source of their supply. A high demand for the *human cargo* exists in the countries of the Middle East and, to some extent, in the West. Some countries - like Thailand, Malaysia, Indonesia, Australia, are thriving destinations for sex tourism, which involves a systematic sexual exploitation of women in a commercial scale.

Causes and forms of trafficking

Causes of trafficking are many. But the foremost among them are *poverty, corruption by public officials and a discriminatory social system* that looks upon women as a commodity. In the countries of South Asia that includes India, Nepal and Bangladesh, countless women are victims of poverty, disease and social discrimination. If, in such a condition, the main income-earning member of a family gets incapacitated or dies leaving no male member to fend for the family, the burden of running the family comes down entirely on a female member. Owing to a low level of literacy or being totally illiterate, such women do not possess even minimum skill in any trade or vocation and as a result, the only way that is left for them to earn an income and survive is the selling of their body, which is what happens in most of the cases. They thus become victims of traffickers and pimps.

Modus operandi followed by traffickers are numerous. Some take the pretext of solemnising a fake marriage to gain control on the life of the woman and use her as a sex slave only to sell her away later to a brothel-keeper. From the brothel, which is protected by a human shield of musclemen, she simply cannot come out. In some cases, a poor woman is taken to a country, for example, in the Gulf, with the promise of a good employment in the form of domestic help or a nurse or baby-sitter. Once she reaches the destination, she is not only sexually abused but also tortured with an inhuman load of work and physical assault. Such an atrocious type of slavery accompanied with sexual exploitation sometimes ends up in the murder of the tormentor by the much-harassed woman who feels utterly disgraced with no meaning of life left for her. A trafficked woman, and for that matter a child, is denied human dignity, which is an inalienable right of a human being. It may be mentioned that sometimes even an educated woman falls into the trap of traffickers who then inflict a dangerously sordid life on her. Lured by the hope, for example, of achieving stardom in Bollywood or a high class job somewhere far away from home, young women get lost in a situation from which they do not have a way for escape. Sometimes, traffickers deceive parents of young girls with false promises of well-paid work or marriage to wealthy husbands and take them into their grip. It also happens that the girl is kidnapped or that the parents are in the bondage of debt and give the girl child away in sale to the trafficker. In such circumstances, the girl eventually becomes a prostitute.

The onset of *globalisation* in the late twentieth century has opened up borders of nation states and introduced speedier and easily accessible Internet, mobile/satellite phones, easier means of travels and convenient methods of money transfer. All these have greatly facilitated trafficking of women and the girl child across national boundaries. Factors like gender discrimination in the Asian and African societies, erosion of traditional family values, organised crime that is associated with drug-trafficking, money laundering, etc. sex tourism, armed conflict and the destitution that it causes, natural and man-made disasters, structural inequities in the social system, deceitful 'adoption' of female children, fake marriages, religious superstitions (like the *Devadasi* system) and so on are a great deal responsible for creating favourable conditions for trafficking in and business with female bodies.

Another important aspect of trafficking is the migration of young women from rural areas to cities in search of work. When they are unable to find work in the cities, they fall prey to the traffickers. Bogus promises and other forms of deceptions are used to entice women from family environment in villages to prostitution in the cities. It, for instance, begins with a job in a massage parlour or a beauty parlour or as a baby-sitter.

Traffickers resort to bribing the Police, border guards and other enforcement agencies, who have the responsibility to check and frustrate inter-state and international trafficking of the girl child and women by road, rail and air, so that they do not face a problem in carrying forward their human cargo to the intended destinations. This is the way organised crime flourishes. Trafficking of women is the third highest profit-generating organised crime after illicit drug-trafficking and gun-running across international borders.

Indian experience

Apart from the inter-state trafficking of women within the country, a good number of women from Bangladesh and Nepal are regularly brought to India across the international borders and put to prostitution. The traffickers have an organized system for this purpose. An estimated two million women from India, Bangladesh and Nepal are presently in sex trade in India. [A nation-wide study conducted for the Department of Women and Child Development between 2002 and 2004 says that there are about four million working sex workers in India.] Of these, more than 5,00,000 are below 18 years of age, which means they are 'children' in the eye of law. These hapless women pass their days in the hellish brothels of the Metros and other big cities of India in sub-human conditions in squalor and without any health care worth the name. A good percentage of them have already been suffering from HIV/AIDS and those who haven't are under its threat.

Besides, women from African, East European and Central Asian countries are also there in sex trade in India but their living conditions are not as bad as that of the South Asian women (thanks to the Indian male's preference for everything foreign). High-level prostitution with which foreigners are normally associated is almost invariably connected with abuse and trafficking of drugs. Big money is invariably involved in this type of prostitution.

It has also been found that, of late, prostitution has become 'mobile', shifting from brothels in red-light areas to anonymous locations in the urban areas, offering services to the clients anywhere anytime. Beauty parlours and 'escort services' are some of the faces of prostitution advertised through Internet, newspapers, etc. The sellers in such cases are literate (speaking good English) and charge high fees for their services.

The current trend of indecent representation of female figures in bill boards, TV pictures, movies, fashion shows, beauty contests, reality shows, etc and the marked transformation in the attitude of the educated class in this regard have greatly contributed to the creation of a value system where sex no longer remains a taboo in the public domain. This environment only facilitates sex trade rather openly. The society's indifference to even live-in relationship helps create an atmosphere of permissiveness. Trafficking of women as a part of sex trade, therefore, does no longer evoke a strong protest from the society. Consequently, the law-enforcing machinery also remains indifferent to this explosive social issue. With terrorism, extremist violence, insurgency, white colour crimes, law and order, etc dominating the public domain, the police in India treat the subject of immoral trafficking as of the last priority. The law in India governing immoral traffic in women is slightly cumbersome and makes it difficult to handle trafficking,

Notes and References

A study in Assam

In Assam, like anywhere else, poverty is the main cause that drives young women to prostitution. Here there are no established red light areas except in one or two towns. In fact, these few recognisable red light areas were established during the World War II to cater for the needs of allied soldiers going to the Burma front. It is not known why these areas had been allowed to continue with the trade even after the Independence of the country. Presently, the women in the trade in most of the urban areas in Assam make themselves available to customers through agents. However, freelancing sex workers are also found soliciting individually or in twos/threes in crowded parts of Guwahati city and other towns. The young women in flesh trade operate from private hostels or hotels or even rented houses. Most of them had come from rural areas having had a poverty-stricken background, maybe being deserted by husband or to look after ailing parents or suffering from a similar problem. Mobile phones are made best use of by floating sex workers, as also by those with fixed addresses. Many commute daily from their villages to the towns. Sex workers ordinarily belong to the age group of 14 years to 40 years—with certain exceptions. Nowadays, they dress and present themselves well.

The sex workers have some class differences also, -- some belonging to very poor and illiterate families and catering to truck drivers, street vendors and the like. This class of sex workers, young as they are, does not take any precaution against HIV/AIDS because their clients refuse to use condoms. They are bold enough to accompany the clients to remote places and attend to multiple customers at a stretch. The other class comprises young women who attend 'calls' of rich fast-going customers at expensive hotels, resorts, etc. This category of girls is a good deal educated and 'mod' type. They operate in a rather sophisticated manner and earn quite a lot of money to satisfy their desire for a better life. They get very handsomely paid and are additionally showered with expensive gifts. Ordinary sex workers or even the better-placed call girls in Assam are economically an unorganised segment of the society.

The State of Assam has become a source of supply of young women for the brothels of the big cities in the country. The communities primarily targeted by traffickers for their recruitment are mainly plains tribals, ex-tea-garden tribes and Bangladeshi types. However, other communities are not entirely left out. Girls to be trafficked are picked up and sent by rail or by road to pre-arranged destinations. They are given promises of some good jobs in which they could earn a lot of money. Thus they go with full consent and do not create any hassle for the traffickers. The victims are sent in small groups of three or four or five so that their movement does not arouse suspicion.

A good number of women from the northeastern states of Assam, Manipur, Meghalaya, Nagaland and Arunachal Pradesh go missing every year. Some of them are never traced back. It is therefore reasonable to presume that most of these missing girls eventually land up in prostitution. It is a daunting task to prevent trafficking that takes place in this fashion.

Mumbai is always the biggest destination for trafficked women who have a workable degree of literacy. Foreign trips, for example, to Hong Kong or Singapore or the Gulf, are organised for them from there. An attractive salary is also offered to hoodwink them. The girls compete among themselves to catch such offers. Thus, the metropolis has become a transit point of business for international flesh traders. Besides, Mumbai itself absorbs a good number of trafficked women in its 'pleasure industry'. Dancing at the bars, since banned officially, has long been an earning option. Thus, many of the missing cases of Assam and the rest of the Northeast remain unsolved.

Figures for Assam

Immoral Traffic (Prevention) Act, 1986

Year	Cases registered	Charge sheet filed
1996	23	7
1997	20	8
1998	34	14
1999	5	5
2000	17	10
2001	6	5

2002	24	8
2003	22	13
2004	28	10
2005	25	10
2006	22	5
2007	23	8
2008	26	12
2009	30	17
2010	15	

In 2005, 268 adult women went missing from Assam. The number increased to 434 in 2006, 529 in 2007, 682 in 2008, 813 in 2009, and 550 till July 2010. Further, 1,968 girls have been missing since 2005. The number of missing male children for the period was 1,878. Out of them, the police rescued 671 girls and 609 boys. The remaining 2,566 children remained untraced.

*[Assam CID figures]

Chapter - VI

Role of Protection Officers in Combating Domestic Violence

Nature of Domestic Violence

'All men who love their wives hit them sometimes', says a proverb. And the tragedy is that many wives, not only in underdeveloped Asian countries but also in the developed West, generally endorse the view. 'It is ok to be hit once in a while', some of them are heard saying. In other words, domestic violence has mostly been, to a certain extent, an accepted norm in most of the societies, whether rich or poor, and even in educated ones. Even now, it is only when a woman is repeatedly and seriously affected by her partner's brutality at her matrimonial home that the attention of the modern civil society and the legal system gets drawn to the problem. Small time violence on women is more or less ignored.

International measures

The late 20th century for the first time in the history of human civilization saw the recognition of domestic violence as a violation of women's rights. Beginning with the adoption of the Convention on Elimination of All Forms of Discrimination Against Women (CEDAW) in 1978, there have been several developments at the international level in the form of the Vienna Accord of 1994 and the Beijing Declaration and Platform for Action (1995), etc. to give succour to women tormented in many ways within and without. In India, as a fall out of these developments, section 498A was formally inserted[1] in the Indian Penal Code (IPC) to provide for a clear legal provision to make the infliction by a husband or by members of his family of mental and physical harassment and atrocities on a married woman a punishable offence. Prior to this, domestic violence as such was not even counted as an offence in Indian criminal law.

1 Criminal Amendment Act, 1983.

The coming of a specific law on domestic violence in India

Practical experience gained during a period of nearly two decades (since 1983) showed that the provisions of section 498A IPC being only penal in nature, the measure could not reach out the rock bottom of the problems that the victims of domestic violence faced. It is of no good to the hapless woman if only her tormentor husband or in-laws go to jail for the crimes they commit. Her problems, among other things, are those of immediate shelter, financial upkeepment, custody of her children with whom she is emotionally attached and the wherewithal to fight litigation with her physically and economically more powerful husband and his family. The irony was that despite the penal provision in the IPC (section 498A) being there all these years, women suffered as badly as ever. The enormity of the situation can be gauged from a 2005 UN report, which said that more than two thirds of women in India (nearly 70%) suffered from domestic violence.[2] Significantly, it was also seen that women who own tangible economic assets are less likely to be victims of the crime. The matter was agitated vigorously from a human rights point of view during the last couple of years by social activists, academicians, lawyers, women's action groups and the media and the response of the Government of India came in the form of a separate law to address all aspects of domestic violence and to provide for civil remedies for the same. Thus came the enactment of "The Protection of Women from Domestic Violence Act 2005" (hereinafter mentioned as the Act).

The duties and functions of Protection Officers and the related matters have been encoded in Chapter II of the Act.

Duties and responsibilities of Protection Officers -- implications

Section 9 of the Act has laid down a very heavy set of duties for the Protection Officers (POs). A plain reading of the section indicates the formidable nature and load of the duties and responsibilities that the POs will have to shoulder in due discharge of their duties. To begin with, the PO has, in effect, been designated as an 'assistant' to the Magistrate concerned; in other words, he has to always remain available to rush at the call of the Magistrate to carry out the latter's instructions so far as any case of domestic violence is concerned. This by itself is a full time job.

2 *Indian Express*, October 13, 2005. However, according to the latest National Family Health Survey, 37 per cent of women in India face domestic violence.

Second, it has been made obligatory for the PO to forward a copy each of the complaints of domestic violence received by him to the magistrate, the Police Station and the available Service Provider (NGO). The PO here is intended to be a bridge between the victim and the authorities. With the PO being immediately available with the legal mandate to help her, the distressed woman is bound to feel a great deal assured. However, when a criminal complaint—that is an FIR-- under section 498A IPC is submitted to the PO rather than directly to the police station, it will be a slightly longer route, which may be a cause of some amount of delay in the initiation of police action in the matter. If the victim has no means for approaching a Police Station, the PO's role in taking the FIR to the police is an absolute necessity. On the other hand, the Magistrate in any case will receive the original copy of the FIR to be sent by the Police Station to the court under the rules and hence the PO forwarding beforehand a copy of the complaint to the former is but a duplication of work. . Only the forwarding (by the PO) of a copy of the complaint to a Service Provider at the initial stage appears to be more relevant. Going into the nitty-gritty of the process provided for here, it is felt that there has to be a functional office for the PO to make copies of complaints received and physically send them over (with a forwarding letter each) to the designated functionaries without delay. This office must function 24x7 with telephone connection, xerox machine, etc for the sake of promptness and efficiency.

Third, the PO has been given the task of moving the Magistrate concerned for issuance of a *protection order* should the victim desire. The PO comes immediately into the picture in such a situation and will have to take initiative to move the court after obtaining a written application to that effect from the victim. But before the magistrate issues a protection order, he will have to observe certain formalities like hearing the aggrieved lady and the offender in person besides witnesses. This is the requirement of procedural law. All along the PO has to pursue the matter closely so that the court's orders are received at the earliest.

Fourth, in most of domestic violence cases, women are in need for free legal assistance. The Act lays responsibility on the PO to organise such assistance from the Legal Services Authority concerned. This is easier said than done. Besides the office work involved, the PO has to approach the officials of the Authority with the application signed by the aggrieved person and by his personal approach, convince them of the need for quick action. Once this is done, just a part of the task is achieved. He then will have to brief the lawyer assigned by the Authority for the case in hand and give him the finer points of the litigation. Given the present day anarchic situation everywhere, this will require a lot of running about and patience on the part of the PO. It is felt that the PO should maintain an hour-to-hour diary in this work. He will definitely need a contingency fund for such a task.

Fifth, the PO's office has to maintain a list of service providers, area-wise. This calls for an objective survey so that the really service-oriented NGOs are chosen as distinct from fake ones. The need of the hour is genuineness; otherwise the very objectives of the law will stagger. The approach of the PO here will have to be absolutely impartial and objective.

Sixth, an onerous task has been thrust on the PO by making it obligatory for him to accommodate an aggrieved person in a *shelter home* should she ask for it. The PO has to maintain a personal contact with available shelter homes in his jurisdiction (and even outside it) and should even be able to persuade the authorities of such a home to somehow accommodate the victim woman (and maybe even her minor children) in an urgent case even if there is no seat or place available. It is only a missionary zeal on the part of a PO that can come equal to the task.

Seventh, the PO is expected to have the medical examination of an injured victim done and to obtain and forward the medical report to the magistrate and the police station – a job that is ordinarily performed by the police. Here it is not only the question of transport and manpower that are required for carrying the victim to and back from hospital but also that of the expertise required to secure the medical reports from the government hospital concerned – a task even the police find difficult to achieve in countless cases owing to non-cooperation from doctors concerned. But to begin with, the PO, in order to be able to act in an emergency situation, must have enough funds on hand to hire a vehicle and manpower for the purposes mentioned.

Finally, the PO has been tasked "to ensure that the order for monetary relief under section 20 is complied with and executed in accordance with the procedure prescribed under the CrPC 1973". On the other hand, section 20 by itself is a composite self-contained provision where the procedure for execution of the court order has been elaborately laid down. It can therefore be reasonably presumed that the main intent of this provision is to put the PO in pursuit, so that in the event of unnecessary delay in the execution process, he can assertively ask the officials concerned to take proper steps or else the negligence will be brought to the notice of the court.

Infrastructure necessary

All the above points sum up broadly the dedicated approach that the PO has to have while dealing with the problems of domestic violence. But it has also to be realised that the PO has also to be provided with the necessary wherewithal to enable him to succeed in his mission. His minimum requirements are summarised below:

1. A small office with a staff and other basic infrastructure, communication facilities, etc.
2. A contingency fund to enable the PO to hire a vehicle or a few helpers or to buy food, cloth, etc for the victim at a short notice.
3. The PO himself should be mobile to be able to run to and fro as between his office and the police station, the hospital, the court, the advocate's chamber, the NGOs' place and so on.

Three very relevant points in respect of appointment of POs emerge here:

(i) Gazetted rank

Considering the type of work that has been assigned to the POs under the Act, they can accomplish their tasks only in collaboration with other official and non-official agencies at pretty senior levels. For this purpose, they will have to develop liaison with very senior people. Therefore, it is felt that the PO should be of the status of a gazetted officer of the government to make his work smooth and easy.[3]

(ii) Not too large jurisdiction

With the continuously rising graph of domestic violence cases in the country, the jurisdiction of a PO should be kept limited to a police circle or sub-division[4] so that he is able to attend properly to all the cases reported.

3 West Bengal is learnt to have appointed independent POs by creating new gazetted posts for the purpose.

4 A police circle or sub-division has normally under it just a few police stations.

(iii) Training

As section 9 of the Act would show, the PO is expected to deal with cases of domestic violence at different stages and in their civil and criminal facets. This means a PO has to have full knowledge of the principles of law, procedures in and requirements of investigation, court procedures, rights of women under the Act as well as other laws for the time being in force, essential medical matters involved in physical violence, male psychology giving birth to domestic violence, etc and should also possess the ability to get remedial things done. All this can be achieved only through an excellent course of training, which could be organised specially for POs by the Ministries concerned of both the Central and the State governments.

The problem in India is that our laws are never implemented in their true spirit owing to bias, negligence and ignorance on the part of different actors in the field. To make the laws work, there need be a coordinated response from various agencies involved. The POs are mandated to become watchdogs in the process of the implementation of the domestic violence law and are intended to take requisite steps in this regard. Among the essential subjects/topics in which the POs should acquire workable knowledge, the following appear to be very important:

Of Laws

International Conventions like CEDAW, Vienna Accord, Beijing Declaration, relevant provisions of the Constitution of India, IPC, CrPC, Evidence Act, Protection of Women from Domestic Violence Act 2005, Dowry Prohibition Act 1961, Protection of Human Rights Act 1993, Immoral Traffic (P) Act 1956, Juvenile Justice (Protection of Children) Act 2000.

Of police investigation

Essential knowledge about dying declaration, inquest on a dead body, injury report, post-mortem report, forensic evidence, DNA fingerprinting, service of summons and execution of warrant, arrest and bail including anticipatory bail, information to the victim about the progress of investigation, procedure to implement 'protection order' and order for monetary benefit to the victim issued by the court, recording of confession of the accused and statements of the victim and important witnesses by a judicial magistrate under section 164 CrPC, and so on.[5]

Of sociological and other aspects

Basic causes and pattern of wife abuse, psychological, educational and economic profile of the abuser, practices relating to dowry, influence of the immediate family on the abuser, alcoholism and substance abuse, and consequential child abuse, value system among the abuser's social connections, state of health care in the family involved, etc.

Ordinarily, the POs will have to address the following problems while tackling cases of domestic violence on spouse and children:

1. Husband's and in-law's coercive behaviour, husband's act of forcing the wife and even children to starve and to remain without proper clothes, minor to serious physical assault, deprivation of medical help, marital rape, attempt to murder, abetment to suicide, murder and covering it up as suicide.
2. Intimidation, striking of an enervating fear in wife's mind, forcing her isolation from neighbours, parents and relations, emotional blackmailing.
3. Verbal abuse; intolerance in day-to-day life; humiliation, degradation and violation of dignity of wife in presence of others. In most of these cases, the man is unaware of the impact of his behaviour.

On the wife's side, the reasons or provocations (justified or otherwise) that are normally seen are as follows:

1. Inability or unwillingness to bring dowry as demanded or expected,
2. Allegedly neglecting in-laws,
3. Going out without telling husband or in-laws,
4. Arguing with husband or in-laws,
5. Refusal to have sex or to respond to sexual fantasies,

---

5 Finer points like the retrospective applicability of the POWFDV Act (under section 26 of the Act) are of very high importance, which need to be taken care of by POs. This is possible only if they acquire an in-depth knowledge of the relevant provisions of law and follow them up properly.

6. Not preparing food as desired and on time,
7. Talking with other males,
8. Extra-marital relations,
9. Compulsive nagging.

The PO cannot be expected to function in a vacuum. A study by the Centre for Advocacy and Research at Pune has shown that facilities for psychological counselling, medical help, shelter homes, etc are yet to be actively developed in Maharashtra. This state of affairs holds good in practically all the states in India. In the absence of necessary facilities, the POs cannot do miracles. The main crunch appears to be financial and organisational. Presently, it is the shortage of funds that holds back training of POs and NGOs and sensitisation programmes for police and judicial officers in the matter of justice to the sufferers of domestic violence. At the same time, infrastructure development for the intended system has also been very slow. Thus, the tenets of the Act are not fully understood and less seriously implemented. Because of lack of awareness programmes for the target groups, only a few among those for whose benefit the law has been enacted in the first place are aware of its existence. Thus, spreading awareness among all is also a job the POs have to do.

Initiative of POs

The POs have to be absolutely fearless in their mission. Section 30 of the Act has declared the POs and the Service Providers as *public servants*, which protects them against vexatious litigation by interested parties. Moreover, in the event of Magistrate's court failing in the perception of an aggrieved woman to deliver proper justice to her, the PO can initiate a proposal to the Legal Services Authority to direct the advocate appointed in the case to file an appeal in the Court of Sessions. Even in the case of breach by the respondent husband (or by his family members) of the protection order passed by the court, the PO has to pursue with the police for immediate action since such a breach of court order is a *cognizable and non-bailable offence.* Therefore, it is a matter of the PO's tenacity that will go a long way to actually ensure delivery by the legal system of justice to battered women.

Chapter - VII

Sexual Harassment at Workplace
(Vishaka vs State of Rajasthan, 1997)

Definition

Sexual harassment is an unwelcome sexually determined behaviour and includes (1) physical contacts and advances, (2) a demand for sexual favour, (3) sexually coloured remarks, (4) exhibition of pornography, and (4) other verbal/non-verbal conduct of sexual connotation. Even suggestive language without bodily contact will amount to sexual harassment. It comes in the form of sexually oriented jokes, comments or an act of teasing on private life, violation of privacy, persistent social invitations or telephone calls, stalking in the office itself, hints of preferential treatment in exchange for sex, etc. The perpetrator of the offence is always a man and the victim a woman.

There is no law yet in the statute book in India[1] on sexual harassment at work place except the ruling of the Supreme Court in the Vishaka case. Till such time a regular legislation on the subject is passed by the Parliament, this ruling stands as the standing law.

Incidence of sexual harassment

Studies have indicated that a good number of the perpetrators of sexual harassment on women employees are their co-workers at the workplace. The next set of people who harass women sexually are their immediate superiors. The official superior normally seeks to buy silence of the victim by application (or by the threat of application)

---

1 A proposal on the enactment of a regular legislation on the subject is pending before the Central Government for quite sometime now. According to the US Equal Employment Opportunity Commission, sexual harassment is a form of sex discrimination that violates Title VII of the US Civil Rights Act of 1964. As per the norms in the US the victim or the harasser may be a man or a woman either way; but in India, the victim has to be a woman while the harasser a man.

of his official power to her disadvantage. In many cases, unobliging women face discrimination in the matter of promotions, important assignments, work load, etc. They also are made to look discredited in office matters as a punishment for failing to oblige the tormentor in his unjust demands. Even a hostile environment is created for her in the office, resulting in colleagues shunning her company to avoid the boss' wrath. On the other hand, higher officials tend to cover up the incident of such harassment to the best of their ability.

Things are pretty bad on this front. Urban working women have now learnt to treat such harassment as a professional hazard. A feeling has come to stay that one should sulk in order to cope with the problem or leave the job if it turns to be too difficult. Sexual harassment is so much in the system now that it sometimes commences right at the job interview itself when the male interviewer makes some advances to the female candidate who is being interviewed.

Summary of the orders of the Supreme Court in the Vishaka case

The apex court has ordered the employers and the persons in charge of workplaces (that will include all public and private establishments) to take the following steps:

1. Orders prohibiting sexual harassment should be publicly circulated at the work place. The term 'workplace' will include all public and private places of work. Even shops, factories and commercial establishments employing more than 10 employees will have to issue the said orders.
2. The conduct rules of the service or the establishment, whether governmental or private, should provide for punishment of persons found guilty of causing sexual harassment to women.
3. Private employers should issue standing orders under Industrial Employment (Standing Orders) Act, 1946.
4. Appropriate conditions should be provided to women workers for leisure, health and hygiene.
5. There should be a complaint mechanism in the organisation. It would be mandatory for the authorities of all public and private offices and establishments with more than 10 employees to set up a complaint committee to look into allegations of sexual harassment. The committee should include a special counsellor.

6. The committee is to be headed by a woman and at least half its members should also be women.
7. A third party representative (maybe from an NGO) should be there in the committee.
8. When conduct of an employee amounts sexual harassment, the committee should take action to punish the guilty.
9. The subject should be affirmatively discussed in employer-employee meetings.
10. Where such conduct amounts to a specific offence under the law, the authorities or the employer shall initiate legal action.
11. The employer has to ensure that the victim or witnesses are not victimised. If necessary, the perpetrator may be transferred out of the establishment.
12. The victim will also have the option of having a transfer from the establishment to get out of the reach of the unwanted persons.
13. The employer must offer all assistance to a victim of sexual harassment.

These guidelines are binding and enforceable in law. However, since these guidelines were not made applicable to educational institutions at the time they were issued, incidents of sexual harassment kept taking place at these places. The Supreme Court has, therefore, come up with a fresh set of directions in this regard. A bench headed by the Chief Justice KG Balakrishnan has said as follows:[2]

"The intention should be to create a situation where such incidents of harassment are *prevented* (italics the author's) and not wait to take action after they have happened. The effort should be to prevent such anti-social occurrences."

The unorganised sector

The Supreme Court orders and guidelines mentioned above, however, do not reach out the women working in the unorganised sector. The question remains 'who will set up the complaints committees in the unorganised sector?'[3] The tragedy of the situation is that the

2 Petition filed by Medha Kotwal Lele, a teacher and victim of sexual harassment [The Telegraph, January 30, 2009].

3 Any future legislation on the subject should address the question and provide for a mechanism.

majority of women workers in India work in the unorganised sector, for example as daily wage-earners, domestic helps, contract labour on construction sites, and so on. The latter set of women has to take sexual harassment meted out to them in their stride. Many a time, they have to suffer molestation, rape, etc virtually without any protest because they are too poor and weak to raise their voice against such harassment and seek redress. Illiteracy, fear of having a bad name and ignorance of remedies available also contribute to their silence in the matter. Here social consciousness about the evil and help from non-official organisations can go a long way to provide succour to the victims. The police should also get sensitised.

It is to be remembered here that the act of delving into the past employment history of the complainant and indulging in unnecessary speculation about her morals are only a way of trying to perpetuate injustice on the victim. Each complaint of harassment requires an in- depth examination of its merits and action should be initiated accordingly.

Action by the police

Sexual harassment at workplace may require the intervention of the police if it turns out to be acute in respect of an individual woman. In such a situation, the police will have to take up a regular case and investigate. Probable sections of law will be section 294, 354 and 509 IPC. The latter two sections are cognizable. Besides, the conduct of the offender may also attract provisions of law in respect of wrongful confinement, public nuisance, and attempt to assault, etc according as the circumstances in the case will indicate.

In a case of sexual harassment, one of the points raised on behalf of the accused was that since there was delay in filing the complaint, the testimony of the complainant was concocted. Rejecting the contention, the Supreme Court has held that since the victim was away from her family, it was natural for her to take some time before deciding on the suitable course of action.

What should the victim do in a case of sexual harassment?

Her first step should be to ask the offender to stop. The victim should shake off any imaginary fear she may have of any adverse fall out of her stand against the harassment she faces and be firm and clear in her reactions to make it obvious to the harasser that she regarded his conduct as offensive and would not tolerate it.

Even as she initiates action against the offender, she should keep documenting in details everything that takes place, noting the time, place, circumstances, etc. Nothing should be left to memory. Copies of relevant papers, cards, *e*-mails, etc should be collected in a File or Folder as a record of evidence. She has also to confide the developments to one or more neutral persons, so that they could give testimony later in any formal enquiry.

If the harasser fails to stop his offensive behaviour with the lady, she should notify her employer without delay about the harassment or danger she was facing. The office, whether governmental or private, is supposed to have an operating mechanism and machinery to go into cases of sexual harassment and take appropriate action. As soon as the victim approaches the authorities, the whole thing gets activated. She, therefore, has to pursue diligently the process of redressal that starts and bring it to a logical conclusion.

All this, however, does not preclude her filing an FIR with the police for action under the criminal law. There are, at the same time, remedies available to her under the civil law.

Responsibility of the Employers

The Supreme Court has, by implication, created in the Vishaka case two sets of responsibilities for all employers:

One, if a case of sexual harassment takes place at a workplace, the employer or the head of office concerned, in order to defend himself, has to show that he had taken reasonable amount of care to prevent the occurrence and did all that was possible to correct the behaviour of the offender.

Two, the employer or the head of office must also show that the victim had unreasonably failed to avail herself of the preventive or corrective measures in force in the establishment.

Thus, the matter creates a triangular burden on the employer, the victim and the offender.

Chapter - VIII

Custodial Violence

What is custodial violence?

Any physical assault made or caused to be made on the body of a person taken into custody by a law-enforcing authority[1] is custodial violence. Such custody may or may not have been lawful in the first place. If the detention of the person was unlawful to begin with, the officer of the state inflicting violence on the detainee is doubly guilty. Even if the detention is legal, it does not permit the officer concerned to physically violate the sanctity of the human body on the pretext of finding out the truth in a given investigation. Physical violence negates the fundamental right to life and liberty and cannot be a part of investigation.

Characteristics

Custodial violence resulting in death is custodial death. Whether or not such violence results in death, it is reprehensible. It is against the very foundation of the principle of rule of law. It is not only arbitrary, but also criminal. A police officer or any other officer of the state who uses violence against an alleged offender in his custody is himself an offender and deserves to be dealt with under the law.

Studies have shown that the pattern of custodial violence in all the States (which includes Union Territories) in India is more or less uniform and it is therefore possible to generalise the nature of such violence. It is a major issue that involves the question of human rights.

---

1 The Police, State CID, State Excise Department, Forest Department, the Army, Para-military Forces and various investigating agencies of the Central Government, like the CBI, the DRI, the Customs and Central Excise and the Narcotics Control Bureau, who have the power to effect arrest and/or prosecute, are all law-enforcing agencies.

The factors found common in custodial violence in India are that

(i) the victims are invariably poor,

(ii) there are no real proofs of their involvement in a crime but only a vague suspicion,

(iii) most of them are held in custody illegally,

(iv) most of them were accused of petty offences.

(v) Police officers guilty of causing custodial death almost always give very funny explanations and do not even know how to cover their trail and therefore it is not very difficult to find out the circumstances and the perpetrators of such deaths or violence.

A judge of the US Supreme Court had remarked, "The police reflect the state and the state the society. If the government becomes the law-breaker, it breeds contempt for law. It invites every man to become a law unto himself; it invites anarchy." Nothing is truer than this statement. Thus, the police have to be fully accountable for the state of health of the person taken into custody by them. What they do with the arrested person has to be transparent.

Common causes of custodial death

(i) The police try to extract 'confession' from the person in custody by application of physical force in the form of prolonged assault or torture.

(ii) The victim is mostly on informal arrest and so the police officer concerned feels a great deal free to use physical force on him.[2]

(iii) Third degree method is used regardless of the state of health of the accused victim.

(iv) Sadistic pleasure is found by some individual policemen in the plight of a tortured victim. Sometimes an orgy of violence takes place at the police station, which is participated in by many.

(v) Individual officer's total disregard for the constitutional and legal rights of the victim.[3]

---

2 Most often the police officer concerned is under intoxication and therefore loses all sensibility while committing violence on a person in custody. Thus, though unintended, death results in such an event.

3 This is compounded by the silence maintained by other policemen on the custodial violence inflicted on the arrestee, though they may not be really approving of the illegal act.

(vi) The investigating officer seeks to solve a crime in a short-cut method avoiding painstaking scientific investigation.

(vii) The officer responsible for the custodial violence feels certain that he would get support of his senior officers or the magistrate concerned in hushing up the crime even if he faces the mandatory enquiry following a custodial death.

(viii) Senior officers or magistrates often conduct superficial enquiries, either administrative or under Section 176 CrPC, accepting the versions of the guilty police officers and the false records prepared by them. Such precedents embolden some policemen to practise violence on persons in custody.

(ix) Lack of supervision by senior officers on the working of police stations/outposts leads to the adoption of arbitrary practices by some junior officers at the police station/outpost level.

(x) Many a time, criminal negligence on the part of police/prison officials concerned in regard to the physical condition of the person in custody leads to unfortunate death in custody.

Outcome of custodial violence

(i) Sensitive men or women tend to commit suicide in the police lock-up itself, especially when mental or physical torture becomes intolerable or they are unable to bear the stigma.

(ii) It brutalises the police force. Innocent persons are framed as a matter of practice.

(iii) Citizens tend to lose faith in the legal system.

(iv) Courts fail to punish the perpetrators of custodial violence since the latter are in a position to tamper with evidence.

(v) Violation of human rights is regularised.

Supreme Court order

The matter of custodial violence that includes assault, torture, rape, sodomy and death in police custody/lock-up/jail custody was dealt with by the Supreme Court in DK Basu *vs* State of West Bengal [WP (crl) No. 539 of 1986] and Ashok Kumar Johri *vs* State of UP [WP (crl) No. 592 of 1987].

This is known as 'custodial jurisprudence'. 'Custodial jurisprudence', as propounded by the apex court, is summarised below:

(a) Custodial violence infringes Article 21 of the Constitution of India and the basic human rights. It therefore strikes a blow at the rule of law.

(b) Assault and torture involves not only physical suffering but also mental agony.

(c) Interrogation, essential as it is, must be carried out by scientific methods.

(d) Third degree methods are totally impermissible.

(e) Balanced approach is needed so that criminals do not go scot-free.

(f) Custodial death is the worst crime in a civilised society. It is pure murder, where the captive victim has no opportunity to defend himself or herself.

(g) State terrorism is no answer to terrorism.

(h) Transparency of action and accountability are two safeguards against abuse of police power.

(i) A victim of custodial violence, and in case of his death, his family members is/are entitled to compensation from the state under the Public Law in addition to remedies under the civil law for damages caused by tortuous acts of police personnel.

(j) Responsibility of all enforcement agencies who have the power to detain a person will be the same as that of the police.

Based on the above propositions, the following requirements have been propounded by the apex court to be followed in all cases of arrest and detention by the police and other enforcement agencies.

Requirements (summarised)

1. Police personnel carrying out arrest and interrogation of an accused person should bear clear identification and name tags.

2. The police officer who effects the arrest of a person shall prepare an Arrest Memo, which shall contain the time and place of arrest and be attested by at least one respectable witness and also signed by the arrestee.

3. The arrestee shall be entitled to have at least one person (who will be interested in his welfare) being informed immediately of his arrest so that necessary help may come.

4. The details of the arrest will have to be immediately communicated by the police to a friend or relative of the arrestee through a legal

aid organisation or the local police if the friend or relative resides outside the town or district where the person was arrested.

5. The arrestee will have to be informed of his rights that he is entitled to during the duration of his arrest.
6. Entries will have to be made in the General Diary of the arrest, the name of the friend or relative informed of the arrest and the particulars of the police officers in whose custody the arrestee was placed.
7. The arrestee should be medically examined at the time of his arrest if he makes a request for the same. Injuries, if any, should be recorded. The Inspection Memo should be signed by the arrestee and the police officer concerned. A copy of the same has to be furnished to the arrestee.
8. The arrestee should be medically examined every 48 hours during his detention. The panel of doctors for the purpose should be one approved by the Director of Health Services concerned.
9. Copies of all documents including the memo of arrest should be submitted to the Magistrate concerned.
10. The arrestee must be allowed to consult his lawyers during interrogation, though not throughout the interrogation.
11. The police officer concerned will intimate the District and the State Control Rooms of the arrest and custody of the arrestee (within 12 hours of the arrest). The control rooms shall display the information on a conspicuous Notice Board.

Failure to comply with the above 'requirements' will invite departmental proceedings and contempt of court proceedings against the police office concerned.

[1997 SCC]

Death due to unhygienic conditions

In another order, the Supreme Court has ruled that death of a detained person due to unhygienic conditions in jail would make officials liable to prosecution for custodial death. This order of the apex court assumes special significance in so far as the charge of custodial death, till now, used to be fastened on the police (or other law-enforcing authorities) only if there was torture or physical assault on the detainee leading to his death.

The ruling came on a petition filed by one Indu Jain and the MP Government who challenged a High Court order that had acquitted certain officials of custodial death charges. The brief of the case was that certain officials attached to the Lok Ayukta of the State had arrested one RK Jain on bribery charges and put him, a known asthma patient, in an unused room that had no ventilation. Jain had an asthma attack due to the dust in the cob-webbed room and he was rushed to hospital in a state of coma. Later in the day, he died.

A bench of Justices A Kabir and M Katju set aside the High Court order and ruled that the officials concerned shall be tried for causing death by negligence.

[*The Times of India*, December 7, 2008]

Role of the National Human Rights Commission

As a safeguard against custodial violence, rape, death etc, the NHRC issued a circular in December 1993 laying down the responsibility of the District Superintendents of Police to report each and every incident of custodial death and rape to the Commission within 48 hours of occurrence.

By another order (No. DG/270/95/716 Dated June 28, 1996), the NHRC has directed that the post-mortem examination of the victims who had died in custody shall be video filmed and the tapes sent to the Commission for scrutiny. This has been done by the NHRC to prevent the doctoring of the PM Reports under the influence of police officials who had perpetrated the crime. The Commission has also circulated a model PM Report (autopsy) Form.

In case of custodial violence including rape and death, the NHRC can hold its own enquiry/investigation if it is not satisfied with the action taken by the state authorities. Such an enquiry/investigation may get initiated on receipt of a complaint or even *suo motu.* The Commission may recommend appropriate action by the state authorities on its findings and even ask for payment of compensation to a victim.

There are many instances of victims of custodial violence or their families getting justice from the initiative of the NHRC ever since its inception.

Chapter - IX

Giving Evidence in Court – IO's Role

Points to Remember

The task ordained for an investigating police officer (IO) is to investigate the case handed to him and find out evidences to prosecute the accused successfully in the court. This means that the labours of the IO will have to undergo the scrutiny of the court, which consists of the presiding judge, the prosecutor and the defence counsel. It happens more often than not that the accused engages more than one defence advocate whose aim would be to demolish the prosecution story. One of the key witnesses for the prosecution in a criminal case is the IO himself, who has a big role in pushing through the case convincingly while the defence tries to punch holes in it .The role of the IO in the court is therefore very crucial. Here are some tips for the I.Os on how to conduct themselves in the court:

1. Do not appear slovenly dressed before a court. A man's personality is partly how he looks and if he can project an impressive personality, his work in the form of investigation done by him also gains weight.

2. Enter the court with dignity when called. Running about, speaking loudly, chewing something and other similar conduct in the court compound give an appearance of a cheap personality, which takes away the trust of all concerned.

3. Have a word with the Public Prosecutor (PP) in advance and clear doubts if any.

4. Do not hang around the court unnecessarily.

5. Go to the court prepared. Refresh your memory from notes, diaries, etc beforehand. To fumble in the witness box is to annoy the court. It destroys the reliability of the officer as a witness.

6. Keep your gaze on the lawyers or the judge as you reply to questions. Do not look away from them or downwards

7. Do not reply to a question unless it is understood clearly. Do not go by guess.

8. Be careful to say simple 'yes' or 'no' to a question, which can well be double-edged. For example, to a question 'have you stopped beating your wife?' if you say yes, it means you used to beat her earlier. If you say no, it means, you continue beating her.

9. Do not lose your temper on provocation by a lawyer on either side. The power of reasoning sinks with the rise of temper. Lawyers many a time provoke the witness and throw him off guard.

10. Be fair and honest. Even if your reply to a question goes in favour of the accused, let it be so but still be fair and honest to the facts of the case. Your duty is to see that justice is done.

11. An officer of the State can claim privilege under the Evidence Act in not replying to a question. Be clear on this so far as it relates to your case.

12. You will sign the written deposition made by you only after it is read over to you and you are satisfied that it has been correctly recorded. You may point out the inaccuracies, if any, for correction.

Points that Come up for Scrutiny at the Court

1. The court scrutinizes the records of investigation to see whether all the vital witnesses have been examined and their statements recorded by the IO. It also takes note of whether seizures had been made of relevant exhibits.

   Where necessary, the statements will have to be recorded under Section 164 CrPC during the investigation to avert some of the witnesses turning hostile later in the trial. It has also to be seen that all the important PWs (Prosecution Witnesses) and relevant exhibits are produced before the court to ensure that there is continuity in the evidence put up for the prosecution story. Failure in taking these steps causes annoyance of the court.

2. Courts are very particular about whether the case diary has been written in the prescribed CD Form maintaining full continuity. It has to be kept in mind that the higher courts are very sensitive on this point. The printed Forms give legitimacy to the Case Diary.

3. The IO's handwriting should be legible and clear for the understanding of the court. There must not be any overwriting or interpolation in the writing.

4. The sketch map should be clearly and cleanly drawn with proper indexes.

5. Seizure Memos are vital documents to prove a case. Clear signatures of witnesses on them are a must. The authenticity of these Memos should not come under doubt. The IO must give over a copy of the Seizure Memo to the person from whom seizures were made so that when questioned in the court, he admits having received it.

6. Test Identification Parade (TIP) of suspects is a means to identify the offender when he is unknown. Great care has therefore to be taken during a TIP so that its genuineness is not questioned later. An improperly done TIP amounts to the framing of a person as an accused and this takes away the trustworthiness of the entire investigation.

7. Expert opinion plays a very important role for the investigator and the court to arrive at the correct conclusion about an incident. The IO therefore has to take all the care to promptly send the exhibits in question to the experts concerned, be it the forensic scientist, or the explosives expert, or one in any other line. Similarly, in the matter of a post mortem examination or a medical examination, the IO should make a specific reference to the expert about the points for determination leaving no scope for ambiguity later. At the same time, if it is required to preserve some materials or ingredients from the exhibit or the body of a person, for example a vaginal swab or bone marrow for DNA test later, the IO should clearly state this in his reference so that there is no bungling in the matter at the expert's end. The I.O should be very clear in his mind as to the nature of examination required and also as to whom to refer to for such examination. In a half-baked investigation where some bungling had taken place, the defence takes full advantage of the situation even though the case was extremely heinous and evidentially strong.

8. There should not be any delay in filing the FIR. However, if there be any unavoidable delay in this owing to some strong reasons, the same should be recorded properly. The co-relation between the FIR and the 'General Diary' entries on a case must be maintained meticulously. Many serious cases end up in acquittal owing to discrepancy in this.

9. It is a common complaint of courts that the full names and addresses of the witnesses (including those of official witnesses like the medical officer, the forensic expert, the RBI officer, the

explosive expert and so on) as well as the IO are not properly recorded in the case diary and the charge-sheet and as a result, it takes a lot of time to trace them and get them to the court to testify in the case, leading to unnecessary pendency and annoyance of all concerned. This situation must be avoided.

10. A similar situation is created when the seized exhibits are not produced at the court on time. This lapse or negligence goes only to the advantage of the accused. The officer concerned in the police station must therefore keep the exhibits in proper order to be able to produce them at the court at a short notice.

11. It has to be seen that only the officer authorised by law investigates the case that is reported. For example, only a deputy superintendent of police or a specially notified inspector of police should take up the investigation of a case under IT (P) Act and not a sub-inspector. Any error in this will result in failure of the case.

12. It sometimes happens that a case is investigated by more than one IO, one after the other. Here the last IO who completes the investigation has to finally see that all the major points in the case have been taken care of, so that it goes to the court as a finished product, and not as a half-baked package.

13. It should be ensured that there is no procedural error during the investigation and at the time of finalizing the charges. For example, when sanction for prosecution is required under Section 196 or 197 of the CrPC, the same shall be obtained from the authority concerned and filed along with the charge-sheet. The prosecution sanction, where it has been provided for, is the basic requirement for the court to take cognisance of the offence and start the judicial process. Any discrepancy between the story given in the charge-sheet and the story given in the sanction for prosecution will lead to the discharge of the accused in the case right away.

14. When a charge-sheet is proposed to be filed under Section 173 CrPC, it must be accompanied with all the relevant papers that will in totality prove the case and based on which the conclusion has been arrived at by the IO Even if just one paper is missing, it is likely to prove fatal for the case.

15. In major cases, witnesses sometimes avoid appearing at the court for deposing in the case, or alternatively turn hostile while giving testimony. All this happens because of intimidation and strong-arm tactics resorted to by the other party. Courts become wary of this kind of problem. Naturally, the police have to take the blame.

Here comes the need for protection of witnesses, which should be ensured as and when necessary, right from the beginning. Where circumstances require, the police should oppose the bail petition of the accused tooth and nail and even move higher courts for cancellation of the bail if already granted by the lower court.

Chapter - X

Legal Aid and Lok Adalat

The Present Law on Legal Aid

The Preamble and Article 14[1] of the Constitution of India have laid emphasis on the principle of equal justice to all, whether rich or poor, irrespective of caste, creed, gender, etc.

Under the Directive Principles of State Policy in the Constitution, Article 38 and 39 provide that the State shall strive to promote a social order in which justice - political, social and economic - is made available to all.

However, the poor and the weak in India understandably cannot have the desired access to equal justice since they cannot afford the expenses involved in the legal processes.

To mitigate this problem, Article 39A, added after an amendment of the Constitution, now provides for an arrangement of free legal aid to whosoever needs it.

The CrPC (Code of Criminal Procedure) and the CPC (Civil Procedure Code) do contain provisions in regard to free legal aid. Section 304(I) of CrPC provides that the Court of Sessions shall assign a lawyer at the expense of the state to a person who is unable to afford one during his trial at the court. Similarly, in a civil case also, Order XXXIII of CPC provides for assignment of a lawyer to a person who applies to the court to be treated as an indigent litigant. Payment of court fee may also be condoned in respect of such a person.

However, it was felt that the matter of free legal aid to poor litigants should be simplified by an independent enactment. Thus,

---

1 Article 14 confers the Right to Equality. It is a Fundamental Right enforceable in law.

in pursuance of Article 39A, the Legal Services Authorities Act 1987 has been enacted to provide free and competent legal services to the weaker sections of the society. Right to free legal aid is now considered a part of the right to life and liberty (Article 21).

The 1987 Act has provided for creation of Legal Services Authorities at the national, state and district levels. It also provides for the same at the High Courts and the Supreme Court.

The prime functions of the Legal Services Authorities at different levels are

1. To formulate policies regarding legal services,
2. To utilise funds at their disposal,
3. To organize legal aid camps,
4. To set up Lok Adalats,
5. To impart legal awareness,
6. To enlist support of voluntary organisations for rendering legal services.

Ordinarily, the following categories of persons, among others, are entitled to free legal aid:

1. A financially distressed member of sc/st,
2. A victim of trafficking/a bonded labourer,
3. A woman or a child in distress,
4. A disabled person,
5. A victim of natural disaster/ethnic or other kind of violence,
6. A workman earning very low wages,
7. An inmate of a protective home,
8. A person with a very low income or no income

It is the duty of the District Legal Services Authority to perform such functions of the State Authority as may be delegated to it from time to time.

Lok Adalat

The Legal Services Authorities Act, 1987 provides that the concerned Legal Services Authority at any level may organise Lok Adalats to promote justice on the basis of equal opportunity. The Lok Adalats provide justice speedily at less expense.

The authority concerned may organise a Lok Adalat at such intervals and places as it thinks fit.

A Lok Adalat consists of a serving or a retired judicial officer and some other qualified persons.

It shall have the jurisdiction to determine and arrive at a compromise or settlement between two or more parties to a dispute in respect of a case either pending or new. In criminal matters, the Lok Adalat can deal with only compoundable offences. It can also exercise jurisdiction over disputes relating to public utility services.

A Lok Adalat can take cognizance of a case on reference from a court based on an application of one of the parties, provided the other party is given an opportunity of being heard on the issue of such reference. The compromise or settlement is to be arrived at on the basis of the principles of justice, equity and fair play.

If no compromise is reached, the case will be sent back from the Lok Adalat to the appropriate court.

The award given by a Lok Adalat has the force of a decree or final order of a court. It is not appealable.

The Lok Adalat has all the powers of a civil court (i) to summon witnesses, (ii) to order production of documents, (iii) to receive evidence on affidavits, (iv) to requisition any public record.

It is expected that the operation of Lok Adalats will drastically reduce the pendency of minor cases in courts.

Chapter - XI

Organised Crime

Organised crime defined

Crime is an act, which violates law. Organised crime is a systematic and continuous violation of law by a group of persons duly organised and disciplined with a view to making profit or monetary gain. Organised crime groups choose selected fields of activity and control the market or even a given territory.

Characteristics of the crime

The tools of operation in organised crimes, among other things, are intimidation, violence and money that corrupts. The *modus operandi* of the actors or 'dons' involved in the crime is to do their work by putting up a facet of legitimate activity and keeping the law enforcement agencies, including the police, on their side through the use of corrupting influences. In present day India, they enlist the support of politicians and other vested interests because that makes their operations smooth and easy.

In major organised crimes, the groups operate globally, with international criminal links. Drugs, arms, gold, human trafficking, etc are some of the objects of interest for the organised crime groups. The difference in laws, attitudes and foreign trade policies of different countries makes it easy for these organised criminals to operate and when necessary, to flee from one country to another to escape action.

Organised crime generates a high-income turn over. This, in turn, enables the induction of sophisticated professionalism in the operation. The actors thus learn to operate with speed, surprise and a high degree of efficiency. Anonymity and secrecy are two fundamental *mantras* for organised crime. .

The operation is hierarchic. The operatives have strict and mutually exclusive divisions of labour. The left hand does not know what the right hand does. Ruthlessness is an essential characteristic of the operation. The operatives are merchants of death and destruction. Collectively the gangsters are known as 'the underworld' and the leaders are called 'dons'. For them, 'the only valuable thing is wealth and the most worthless thing is the life of others.'

Classification

There are three types of organised crime groups, *viz.*

1. Criminal Gang
2. Crime Syndicate
3. Criminal Racket

Gangs of dacoits, kidnappers, smugglers, pickpockets and similar groups fall into the first group. The present day terrorist groups also fit into this category.

Crime syndicates provide forbidden or illegal service to customers who are prepared to pay for the same lavishly. Gambling, boot-legging, prostitution, drug-trafficking, etc fall in this category.

Racketeering involves the giving of some illegal service to clients who are desirous of making payments for the same to be able, in their turn, to make higher profits. For example, theft of crude oil from oil storage depots and tankers and selling the same to businessmen-receivers in a regular way amounts to racketeering in crude oil.

Mafias operate crime syndicates or rackets in their own style and develop methodology peculiar to individual groups and their leaders. They maintain co-operation among themselves and win over politicians and powerful government officers to make their functioning smooth and easy.

Strategy for investigation of organised crime

In order to cause effective investigation of organised crimes, the following mode of action is required:

1. Specialised investigating teams should be formed. Specialisation will be required for such teams in each field of organised crimes, e.g., drug-trafficking, gun-running, money-laundering, boot-legging, oil-pilferage, smuggling of timber and other forest products, theft

of Railway property, and so on. All the team members should possess special capability in their respective fields.

2. There shall be a data bank in respect of each of the various branches of organised crime. Data have to be kept updated regarding new members joining the gang concerned, their crime profile, new receivers coming into the fray, fresh acquisition of properties by them, fine tuning of *modus-operandi* by them, etc

3. Net working of criminal intelligence is a must. The police should be able to penetrate the labyrinth of the criminal organisation concerned and has to have the means to cross check the information collected. Advance intelligence is the life-blood of any effort to curb organised crime. At the same, sharing of intelligence with other police agencies has to be arranged so that new inputs are available for concerted action.

4. The investigators have to be young and able-bodied. Their integrity has to be above board. They have to be specially trained. They should not suffer from the dearth of modern equipments and logistic support. Preferably they should have an assured tenure so as to be able to acquire higher and still higher degree of expertise in a given field.

5. A multi disciplinary approach is required to deal with organised crimes. Departments like Customs, Excise (both central and state), Enforcement, Income Tax, Forest, Petroleum, Railways, Transport, etc, apart from the Police, should be caused to be involved in the drive to combat organised crimes.

6. Considering how intense the organised crimes in question are, the government may enact a special law to deal with them. Ordinarily, it should be possible for the police to handle an organised crime with the existing laws like IPC and other special laws in the statute book. Section 120B of IPC has a very wide application in the said crime.

7. Proper prosecution of organised criminals is as important as investigation. It also needs a high degree of professional competence on the part of prosecutors. If necessary, special public prosecutors will have to be appointed to deal with the cases. The question of protection of witnesses in the cases concerned has also to be kept in mind.

8. Preventive detention law is a good instrument to deal with organised crimes. The police should liberally make use of such

a law to cripple such criminals in their unlawful activities. Once there is a break in the criminal activities of a gang, its working system gets disorganised and concerted action by the authorities at this juncture will throw them off the path of their venture.

Chapter - XII

Community Policing

'Community policing' is a concept of policing that is done with the active involvement of the entire community for whose benefit policing is, in the first place, intended to be done. It is a kind of police-public partnership. The concept is not new. Advanced countries had adopted the idea way back in the 1960s and 1970s. Countries like the USA, the UK, Japan, Germany and many others have put the concept into practice, replacing more or less the earlier 'Beat Police' system. The earlier system provided that the Beat Police should know the local residents personally so far as possible and perform policing duty. The residents of the beat did not practically have a role or participation in it. Now, in community policing, the local residents or the community have a positive role to play and to be friends and guides to the police. It is policing by mutual co-operation.

Key Features

1. Community policing involves a programme of regular interaction between the police and the public.
2. Crime prevention is done by joint participation of both the police and the public, in intelligence gathering and patrolling, etc.
3. The command system is decentralised.
4. There is increased accountability of the police to the local community.
5. There is a shift in emphasis from typical police duties to the rendering of non-police services (in addition to police duties).

Crime prevention and security duties become easier if the police take the local community into confidence. If this is done, the people will turn into the eyes and ears of the police, obviously with a wider reach. They would inform the police in advance whatever comes to their knowledge. This would naturally lessen the burden of the police. Even in the matter of taking preventive measures, the people's co-operation goes a long way to strengthen the hands of the police even in terms of numbers. Investigation of crimes, including arrest and prosecution of offenders, will be less painstaking when the people come forward to assist the police.

Methods

1. To win the confidence of the community, the police will have to get closer to them by showing solidarity in both their happiness and difficulties, even in matters that do not concern the police directly.
2. Police officers at the station level should freely participate in community festivals, ceremonies and other similar things in different localities in their jurisdiction. They should assist the local community in organising and running them. The people appreciate enormously the helping hand that is extended to them in matters of the community's interest and thus a bond of trust is formed. This generates spontaneous co-operation of the people in many more things.
3. The ability of the police to perform duties effectively, Sir Robert Peel had said, is dependent upon public approval of police actions and behaviour. The police must secure the willing and voluntary co-operation of the public in the implementation of law. This is possible only through consultation with the grassroots level of the people.
4. The police should always be prepared to rush to render help to the distressed in even those fields, which do not strictly fall within police duties.
5. The police should always make themselves available to people for consultation and to offer guidance in matters, which concern both. Here the initiative must come from the policemen themselves. In other words, they should be more accessible and communicable. This will help the community to know the police in human terms.
6. The police must maintain transparency in all its dealings with the people. The principle of fairness in their work should be manifest. Integrity of policemen should always be beyond any doubt.

7. People get concerned not only at serious crimes like murder, robbery, rape, etc but also, equally, in low-key troubles in their localities. The important police functionaries of the area concerned should have regular meetings with the people to look into their grievances and sort out their problems. This will also help the police remain abreast of developments in the locality.
8. The police should put in place permanent committees, one in each village or locality, to function on behalf of the local community as a bridge to the police. It shall meet at regular intervals for deliberation and taking decisions on outstanding issues.
9. A Neighbourhood Watch Group should be created to regularly conduct patrolling to prevent crime, especially crimes against property, in its given area. This group may also be authorized to keep track of illegal migrants, inter-district gang of cheats, smugglers of forest products, encroachers on government land, cattle thieves, drug traffickers and so on. One of the briefs for the group should be to monitor the giving and taking of dowry, incidence of domestic violence, abuse of children, employment of child labour and similar socio-economic matters. If such things come to notice, the group shall bring the same to the notice of the police and also of civil officers like the area magistrate or *tehsildar*.

Experimentation of the idea

The experiment in community policing has brought the crime figures down in the USA and Singapore in recent years. People at different places where this scheme has been introduced have reported that they are now less scared of the possibility of crimes taking place than ever before.

In India, states like Andhra Pradesh, Tamil Nadu, West Bengal, Madhya Pradesh, Assam, among others, have adopted the concept of community policing in various ways. Participants in the programme are known by different names in different states, like Friends of Police, Village Defence Society, etc. There have been at least two such programmes in Assam, Aswash and Prahari, which made a significant mark in two very important fields *viz*, (1) assistance to children orphaned in the current armed conflict in the State and (2) prevention of so-called witch-hunting in the interior areas, normally inaccessible to the administration. These two programmes have been able to project a human face of the Assam Police to the common people. The rural folk have now been extending co-operation to the police in much greater degree than before. In the city of Gauhati, Nagarik Samitis - through community participation - had achieved a good deal of success in the late 1990s in the matter of prevention and detection of property crimes.

One of the challenges in this matter is to keep up the interest of the people in the subject. Here, the police have to be innovative and devise various means to sustain the tempo. Organising community sports in a programmed way could be one of the ways to sustain such interest. There could also be a helpline for women in distress, a slum development programme or some such schemes, which could be implemented through the joint participation of the police and the public. At a time when the state police forces are overstretched in various commitments like those in the matter of tackling terrorism, Naxalism, VVIP security, etc. police personnel available for normal police duties are too few. Human resources available in the villages and outlying localities can therefore supplement the manpower of the police in general crime prevention work and create a healthy environment.

Chapter - XIII

Interrogation of Suspects

Interrogation of Suspects

Interrogation is the process of finding out facts and circumstances of a case by questioning the accused persons and suspects in a crime.

It is an intellectual game where the interrogator has to be mentally faster than the suspect, so that he can gather all the requisite information from the suspect regarding the crime. Interrogation is a very important tool for investigation, which has to be artfully used by the investigator.

Qualities of an interrogator

1. Patience.

   [It has to be kept in mind that a suspect is always a slippery character and to deal with him it needs a great amount of patience.]

2. Determination to make a breakthrough.
3. Confidence in himself that he would succeed.
4. Prior knowledge about the details of the crime.

   [The interrogator must be acquainted with facts and circumstances of the crime to be able to confront the suspect on the essential details.]

5. Ability to understand the mind of the suspect.

   [This grows with the experiences that an interrogator keeps gathering over the years.]

Psychological conditions that impact interrogation

1. A guilty person under interrogation is always under psychological pressure. The interrogator has to intensify the pressure.

2. When the suspect is confronted with proven facts and evidences, he finds himself lost and he seeks relief from the situation by stating the truth.
3. The efforts of the interrogator should be to put the suspect on the defensive.
4. It is worthwhile to make the suspect guilt-conscious by emphasising the enormity of the crime committed by him, including its moral and legal implications.

To prepare for interrogation

The following check points should be re-checked before commencing an interrogation session:

1. Whether details of the incident, its background, the possible motive of the perpetrators, and the particulars and antecedents of the accused and the suspects have been collected and taken mental note of by the interrogator before the interrogation session begins;
2. Whether the sitting arrangements ensure privacy;

   [The interrogator should be at the same eye level as that of the suspect and must sit close to him putting the effect of his personality on him. The interrogator should keep observing the psychological movements of the suspect to take advantage of his helplessness.]
3. Whether the interrogator is in plain cloth;

   [The person interrogated feels comfortable in the presence of an interrogator not in uniform. When the interrogator is in plain cloth, the suspect is likely to confide in him his secrets and thereby give clues to the unsolved crime.]
4. Technical aids like tape recorder, video camera, etc should be arranged beforehand and kept concealed;

   [No offender would like to be on record on how and why he had committed an offence, especially when the offence is of a serious nature.]
5. The place of interrogation should not have things, which are likely to distract attention and concentration.

To put it briefly, there should be no one else at the place of interrogation other than the interrogators. It should not be a control room or an office room where people, even policemen, tend to visit frequently for some reason or other. Cell phones, telephone, wireless sets, etc should be barred from there since these are likely to distract attention from the subject of interrogation.

Measures that help attain success in interrogation

The interrogator should not take paper and pencil to the interrogation room at the initial stage. This helps create a congenial atmosphere for the suspect to make a confession.

Alertness should be there to take mental note of what the suspect says in order to confront him later with contradictions. When time is ripe, confession should be promptly recorded.

The interrogator, during his conversations, may show care for the well-being of the suspect's family and inform him of the measures taken to that end. It gives psychological support to the suspect to come up with a revelation.

Interrogation should be done in a slow but steady manner. The interrogator must make enough time available to himself for this purpose. It cannot be done in a hurry when he has a number of other jobs to do.

Physical discomfort felt by the suspect should be removed to put him at ease and make him friendly.

Choice of the interrogator should be such that he is able to interact with the suspect at the latter's intellectual level.

Some useful tips for interrogators

1. The suspect (and his personality) is to be carefully sized up (for example, whether he is of active or passive type)
2. The suspect's strong and weak points should be explored.
3. Bullying and the third degree method are to be totally avoided. Bullying includes taunts and insults.
4. To give an impression that the interrogator is in search of the truth.
5. Promises that cannot be fulfilled should not be made.
6. The interrogator should be assertive so that the suspect comes to understand that it would be futile for him to give a false statement or a statement filled with lies.

7. To appeal to the subject's pride.
8. To remain expressively sympathetic to the subject throughout interrogation.
9. Use the weapon of flattery to a certain extent.
10. The subject is to be made to repeat the entire story of the crime as it emerges at the end of interrogation.
11. It has to be kept in mind that Article 20(3) of the Constitution gives an accused person the right to silence and therefore no one can be coerced to say something that becomes a piece of evidence against himself.

Bottom-line

'*All interrogations must, to some extent, make a suggestion to the witness. It would be perfectly nugatory to ask a witness if he knew anything about something*'.

–Lord Langdale

Chapter - XIV

Quotes in Police Law

Quotes in Police Law

1. Justice delayed is justice denied.
2. Ignorance of law is no excuse.
3. Locard's Exchange Principle

Whenever two sets of material bodies meet, there is a transfer of some materials from one set to the other.

**Criminal investigation should follow this principle, which underscores the fact that in a criminal offence, there is bound to be some clue at the place of occurrence. If the IO has not been able to find one, it shows his lack of competence.*

4. As grammar is to language, so are the police to the society.
5. A police officer is both a citizen and a law enforcement officer.
6. A police officer is a servant of the law.
7. Honesty in thought and deed should characterize a police officer's official and private life.
8. In this country, the only people who will come forward to give evidence against government officers are those who do not mind their houses being burnt, their shops looted, their relatives turned out of government employment, themselves and their families dragged upon false charges and sent to jail.

–Mr Pennel, Sessions Judge in Bengal in 1899.

* *This remark made a century back holds good even today.*

9. If we do not maintain justice, justice will not maintain us.
10. In no sense do I advocate evading or defying the law. That would lead to anarchy.

–Martin Luther King

11. The average life of a terrorist, whether fundamentalist or insurgent, is not more than ten years anywhere in the world.

    –An Indian Army General

12. The police have always been ruler-friendly.

    –Ved Marwah, IPS (Retd)

13. The Judges represent the State and its authority, unlike the bureaucracy and other services. Judicial service is not merely an employment nor are the judges mere employees. A dishonest judicial personage is an oxymoron.

    –The Supreme Court of India.

14. Law is not for the condemned but for the victim.

    [Home Ministry report to the President of India on the mercy plea of Dhananjoy Chatterji who had raped and killed teenager Hetal Parikh. Dhananjoy was later hanged.]

15. Quick convictions are not always healthy.

    –A South African Judge.

16. A person's knowledge of a conspiracy is not enough to implicate him as a member of the conspiracy.

    –DP Wadhwa, J

17. Oath cannot be administered to an accused person.
18. False allegations against a spouse are a cruelty.

    –The Supreme Court.

19. When a Hotel collects from a guest every time he goes out the key to the room, it accepts responsibility for the baggage kept there.
20. A defendant cannot be vexed twice.
21. Fraud and justice cannot dwell together.
22. Motive, overt act and post-crime conduct are enough to deny bail to the accused.
23. Better a diluted sentence than the one that goes against our conscience.
24. A crime is an injury to the State rather than to a private citizen.
25. Right to health is an integral part of the right to life.
26. The more the laws, the less are justice.

    –Cicero

27. Justice should not only be done but also seem to be done.
28. Violence is an acquired behaviour.
29. An Army which fights against the weak becomes weak itself.
30. The nearness of the police to the people they serve is the genuine guarantee against strong-arm methods and their so-called brutality.

–Joginder Singh, IPS (Retd)

31. The rule of law has become a rule of class in India.

–Justice DA Desai

32. A strong Army and an efficient Police are likely to do more for Indian's self esteem and independence than any result that could possibly emerge from 'planning'. The army and the police provide the background for development because they create the condition in which development is possible.

–Jawaharlal Nehru

33. Sir Robert Peel, then Home Secretary of England, had laid down the principles known as Peel's principles, for the police in the UK and the rest of the British empire. The said principles are as much valid now as they were then.

    a. The police must be stable, efficient and militarily organized under government control.
    b. The absence of crime will best prove the efficiency of the police.
    c. Crime news must be widely distributed.
    d. Territorial distribution of the force by hours and shifts must be accomplished.
    e. No quality is more indispensable to an officer than a perfect command of temper; a quiet determined manner has more effect than violent action.
    f. Good appearance commands respect.
    g. Proper training of personnel lies at the root of police efficiency.
    h. Public safety requires that every policeman must be given a number.
    i. The Police headquarters should be centrally located and easily accessible to all people.

j. Policemen should be appointed on probation basis.

k. Police records are necessary for the correct distribution of police strength.

l. The best way to select men is 'to size them up' and find out what their neighbours say about them.

34. The quality of police service will not significantly improve until higher educational requirements are established for its personnel. The complexity of police task is as great as that of any profession. The performance of this task requires more than physical process and common sense. Personnel who in various unpredictable situations are required to make difficult judgments should possess a sound knowledge of society and human behaviour. This can be achieved through advanced education.

–Presidential Commission on the police in the USA, 1967

35. Good laws are as people abide by.

–Aristotle

* *This means that laws should arise as a 'felt need'. Laws should be broadly acceptable in order to be smoothly enforceable.*

36. Even the most ethical and ardent supporter of human dignity does not hesitate to cajole the police to use extra judicial measures when they themselves are in trouble. They have no compunction if the police use violence to help them out against an adversary or a suspect.

* *A double standard indeed.*

37. The police are the best reflection of a society. If the society is tolerant and humane, the police will act accordingly.

–Sir Robert Mark, former London Police Commissioner

38. Crime does not look the same on the street as it does in legislative chamber.

–US presidential commission

* *What about a courtroom?*

39. Functioning under the constraints and handicaps of an outmoded system, the police performance has undoubtedly fallen short of public expectations.

–National Police Commission of India

40 Intelligence is not to make no mistake, but quickly to see how to

make them good.

–Bartlett Brecht

41. There can be no law without order; there can be order without law.
42. For terrorists there are no innocents.
43. No system in the world is human-proof. Men of dubious character can pervert all institutions.
44. Some had to be trusted. Let it be judges.

–Lord Denning

45. If the Minister is of average calibre, he will like to have an officer with a calibre below average.
46. The trouble with making mental note is that the ink fades so fast.
47. No one ever has invented a better intelligence test than matrimony.
48. What distinguishes a revolutionary is not his ability to kill but his readiness to die.

–Trotsky

49. Crime expands according to our willingness to put up with it.

–Berry Farber

50. Justice is too important to be left only to judges.

–Justice VR Krishna Iyer

51. Once paid, the extortionist comes for more.
52. Good cops make bad spies, good spies make bad cops.

–John Deutch, Director of CIA in 1995

53. Be you ever so high, the law is above you.

–Supreme Court of India

54. Silence is half endorsement.
55. Whoever profits from crime is guilty of it.
56. I heard a judge telling a lawyer, 'I know you bring paid witnesses, but why do you bring the same ones each time?'

–Mark Tully

Consumer Rights

(a) Right to choose

(b) Right to be informed

(c) Right to be heard

–John F Kennedy

57. No man of whatever estate or condition that he be, shall be put out of his land or tenement, nor taken nor imprisoned, nor disinherited, nor put to death, without being brought in answer by due process of law.

So 'by due process of law' I mean the measures authorised by the law so as to keep the streams of justice pure; to see that trials and inquiries are fairly conducted; that arrests and searches are properly made; that lawful remedies are readily available; that unnecessary delays are eliminated; It is in these matters that the common law has shown its undoubted genius.

–Lord Denning

58. All interrogations must, to some extent, make a suggestion to the witness. It would be perfectly nugatory to ask a witness if he knew anything about something.

–Lord Langdale

59. Justice has been described as a lady who has been subject to so many miscarriages as to cast serious reflections upon her virtue.

–William L Prosser (the Judicial Humourist 1952)

60. Law is the greatest civilizing machinery. It liberates the desire to build and subdues the desire to destroy. And if war can tear us apart, law can unite us, out of fear or love or reason or all the three. Law is the greatest human invention. All the rest give man mastery over his world, law gives him mastery over him.

–Lyndon B Johnson, former US President

61. Law is founded on common sense.

62. Laws too gentle are seldom obeyed; laws too severe are seldom executed.

–Benjamin Franklin

63. Good laws lead to the making of better ones; bad ones bring in worse.

–Rousseau

64. Laws grind the poor; and rich men rule the law.

–Oliver Goldsmith.

* *It therefore follows that the rich grind the poor through the instrument of law.*

65. Law does change with times and circumstances, and not merely through legislative reforms.

–Frankfurter, Felix [1956]

66. Justice, though due to the accused, is also due to the prosecutor. The concept of fairness must not be strained till it is narrowed to a filament. We are to keep the balance true.

–Benjamin N Cardozo [1934]

67. Nothing should be done which creates a suspicion that there has been an improper interference with the course of justice.

–Lord Hewart [1924]

68. The greatest of all gifts is the power to estimate things at their true worth.

–Francois

69. It is as much the prosecutor's duty to refrain from improper methods calculated to produce a wrongful conviction as it is to use every legitimate means to bring about a just one.

–Sutherland George Berger *vs* US

70. There are many forms of professional misconduct that do not amount to crime.

Chapter - XV

Burden of Proof and Presumption
(In the Law of Evidence)

1. The general rule with regard to the burden of proving a fact is that "he who asserts must prove." This means that the burden of proof lies upon the party, which asserts a fact (or makes a complaint) in the affirmative, and not on the party, which denies it.
2. The concept of burden of proof is understood in two senses:
   a. Firstly, it means establishing the entire case,
   b. Secondly, it involves introducing evidence at any stage of the proceedings.
3. In criminal cases, the basic principle of jurisprudence is that the accused is to be presumed innocent till he is proved guilty. The accused need not produce evidence to prove his innocence. Even when doubt arises as to who was guilty, the benefit goes to the accused.
4. However, when the accused relies upon any of the 'general exceptions' as a plea for his defence, the burden is on him to prove that he fell under any one of the categories mentioned therein. For instance, if someone asserts that he had to kill a person in exercise of his right of private defence, he has to prove that the circumstances were such that unless he had killed the person, the said person would have killed him.
5. In certain instances, the accused commits an offence without leaving any mark or evidence. To combat this problem, our lawmakers have made certain special provisions in the law under which the court may presume the existence of some facts in a given circumstance in certain cases of grave nature. Here the burden shifts from the prosecution to the accused. Sections 111A, 113A, 113B and 114(A) of the Evidence Act deal with the

presumptions which the courts have the liberty to take in coming to a conclusion.

For example, under section 113A of Evidence Act, when the question arises whether the commission of suicide by a woman had been abetted by her husband or any relative of her husband and it is shown that she had committed suicide within a period of seven years from of her marriage and that her husband or such relative of her husband had subjected her to cruelty, the court may presume, having regard to all the other circumstances of the case, that such suicide had been abetted by her husband or by such relative of her husband. The prosecution has to prove the following points here:

a. That the woman who committed suicide was married.

b. That she committed suicide within 7 years of marriage.

c. That she was subjected to cruelty during the subsistence of her marriage till her death or till sometime before her death.

Now, with the above conditions laid out, the court may and should presume that her husband or someone related to him had abetted her suicide. It will now be the burden of the accused to prove that he had not abetted the suicide.

6. (a) Section 111A deals with presumptions during insurgency conditions in a given area.

(b) Section 113A deals with presumptions in cases of suicide by married women.

(c) Section 113B deals with presumptions in cases of dowry death.

(d) Section 114A deals with presumptions in cases of rape.

Chapter - XVI

Juvenile Justice

The Concept

The concept of Juvenile Justice follows from the concept of 'the Rights of the Child'. The present Juvenile Justice Act 2000 (JJ Act) in India is a follow-up of the UN Convention of 1989 on the Rights of the Child.[i] The rights of the child include the basic rights of survival, protection, development and participation.

Juvenile defined

Under the JJ Act 2000, a child and a juvenile are synonymous. Any person who is below 18 years of age is a child; in other words, a juvenile. The present law does not consider a child a criminal even if it had committed an offence that amounts to 'crime'. Such a child is treated as one who is 'in conflict with law' The Act makes a two-fold approach to the problems of the child, viz, a delinquent child and a neglected child.

Law for juvenile offender/neglected child

A child or a juvenile in conflict with law cannot be arrested and detained in a police lock-up or jail in the way an adult is treated for an offence. Such a child is to be given bail by the police themselves at the earliest opportunity so that it does not come in contact with criminals who are found at such places. In a heinous case, the offender child has to be immediately produced before the Juvenile Justice Board of the district constituted for the purpose. The said Board is presided over by a principal magistrate and has two other members taken from among social workers. One of the members shall be a lady.

An under-trial juvenile can be temporarily detained in an 'observation home,' but that should be only with orders from the

JJ Board. If the detention as decided by the Board is to be for a reasonably long term (the purpose being his or her eventual rehabilitation), it shall be done at a 'special home'.

Under Section 63 of the Act, every police station shall have a 'special juvenile police unit' to deal with the cases of juvenile delinquency. At least one police officer at the police station must be designated as a 'juvenile or child welfare officer' to look after the welfare aspect of the neglected child that comes to the notice of the police.

As regards neglected children, the Act provides for a 'Child Welfare Committee' at the district level. A child in need for care and protection may appear or be produced before this committee by a police officer or a social worker or even a private person. Such a child may be given temporary shelter at a 'shelter home' recognised for the purpose. For long-term care, treatment, education, training, development and rehabilitation of a neglected child, there is the provision of 'children's homes' to be run under the control of the social welfare department of the state government.

A child or a juvenile could be a victim of circumstances. He or she may have been a starving orphan, or suffering from malnutrition, may have been an object of sexual abuse, or overworked (and abused) as a child labourer, or sick from some incurable or complicated disease or having fallen in bad company, had taken to crime or drug addiction, alcoholism, etc.

Whatever may have been the reason for his or her distress, the law provides that the child victim has to be taken care of by the state and its various agencies, including the police. Any person or a body of persons, who is, or are, responsible for a child's sufferings will have to be brought to book under the law. At the same time, the child has to be reverted back to normal life. This is a task, which has to be jointly accomplished by the police, the judiciary, social activists who represent the society, other professionals like doctors, lawyers, government servants and last but not the least, the common citizens. However, the family – which, in effect, means the parents at the first instance – has the foremost responsibility to rear a child in a proper form. Most of the time, a broken family leads its children to an irretrievably wrong path.

Rights of the child

Apart from the JJ Act 2000, there are the following laws that safeguard the right of the child to life, liberty and development.

Constitution of India

(i) Article 14 [right to equality]

(ii) Article 19 [fight to freedom of speech, etc.]

(iii) Article 21 [right to life and liberty]

(iv) Article 21A [right to free education up to the age of 14 years]

(v) Article 23 [right against trafficking and forced labour]

(vi) Article 24 [employment of children in factories etc is prohibited]

(vii) Article 39 [tender age of the child is not to be abused but to be protected]

(viii) Article 47 [right to a good standard of living and nutrition]

Factories Act 1948

No child below 14 years can be employed in a factory.

Plantation Act 1951

No child below 12 years can be employed in a plantation.

Mines Act 1952

No child is to be employed in any mining operation.

Motor Transport Workers Act 1961

No child shall be required to work in a motor transport undertaking.

Child Labour (Prohibition and Regulation) Act 1986

It is to ensure general welfare of child labourers.[ii]

Prevention of Disabilities (Equal Opportunities, Protection of Rights and Participation) Act 1995

Among other things, it provides for meeting the needs of children suffering from physical disabilities.

Prevention of Child Marriage Act 2006

It prohibits marriage of a male below 21 years and a female below 18 years.

Probation of Offenders Act 1958

It provides for release of offenders, especially those under 21 years, on probation.

Forms of child abuse

Worldwide there is an awakening that the society and the state must do all that is possible to stop the abuse of the child. Child abuse has countless forms, e.g.

(i) parental abuse,

(ii) institutional abuse,

(iii) corporal punishment, [1]

(iv) abuse by paedophiles,

(v) incest (sexual exploitation by near relations),

(vi) neglect by parents or the guardian,

(vii) indecent representation of the child, particularly of the girl child,

(viii) child prostitution,

(ix) forced labour,

(x) starvation and hunger accompanied with malnourishment and squalor,

(xi) forced begging,

(xii) depriving the child of self-respect and dignity,

(xiii) terrorist attack that upsets the life and home of the child for ever.

(xiv) forced illiteracy, where the child is denied the opportunity to pursue studies.

Initiative by the police

A police officer as a visible representative of the state has a great amount of responsibility towards the implementation of the constitutional and legal provisions meant for the protection of the child. Even at the places where the police officer does not seem to have a direct role, he must come forward to take the requisite initiative to enlist support of the other agencies of the state as well as NGOs (if there are any) and address the problem.

---

1 Many a time corporal punishment meted out by a teacher leads even to death of the child.

Killer kids

Failure of the family or the society to take proper care of a child, particularly of its emotional sides in its earlier years, may result in its becoming a dangerous person and a burden for the society. There are many awe-inspiring stories of killer kids, which the law finds difficult to deal with. Researches have shown different causes for such kids going astray and turning into a serious social problem. Juvenile crimes that include offences ranging from petty theft to extortion, rape, kidnapping for ransom and murder in horrific forms are often reported in the media.[iii] The causes of these crimes, as discerned by experts, are found to flourish in the social life itself. For example, investigation into the rape of a 9-year-old girl by a 12-year-old boy revealed that the boy was watching pornographic DVDs regularly. The question that comes up here is, 'how did the young one have the facility to watch such DVDs?' Similarly, other teen-age acts of violence have their origin in the real-life violence and permissiveness in which the teens live. The rise in substance abuse, alcoholism, attraction to expensive consumer durables, like sophisticated cell phones, digital cameras, luxury cars, etc are contributory factors to teenage crimes in various forms. In most of the teenage crimes, the methods adopted are extremely cruel and depraved.

Given the nature and circumstances of many of such crimes, it becomes a pertinent question as to how to deal with them. The liberal approach of the law of juvenile justice fails to meet the public outrage that follows the commission of such crimes. Some case studies are noted below:

1993

Sajal Barui, 16, of Kolkata, allegedly strangled his father and stepbrother to death, and burnt alive his stepmother.

2003

Five Mumbai collegiates, Ashish Varvale (20), Clinton Fernandez (16), Wilfred Dias (19), Karan Khanna (17) and Clint Fernandez (19) allegedly stabbed Leticia Mendez and her daughter Glenda Lobo, and later hanged Glenda's 18-month-old son from a ceiling fan.

2005

Parveen, a teenager in Murthai village near Sonepet, molested a girl and then shot dead her younger brother when he protested.

13-year-old Delhi boy bludgeoned his friend with a stone after they had a fight.

2006

Three juveniles were arrested at Mangaldoi (Assam) on October 21, 2006 on the basis of circumstantial evidence regarding the brutal murder of one Malekjan Begum, a 7-year-old girl. Her body was earlier found in a jute field with deep cuts on the neck and in a pool of blood.

2007

Three teenagers in Ahmedabad killed Dhyey Khambhu, their six-year-old neighbour. The youngsters wanted to raise Rs 25 lakh in ransom, hoping to lead a life of luxury later on.

Mumbai teenager Adnan Patrawala was killed by a group of four youngsters who demanded a ransom of Rs 2 crore from his wealthy parents.

Saurabh Tribhuban, 16, allegedly strangled Parth Panchal, 9, with a nylon rope and then hid the body in a cupboard in his house in Mumbai.

Such incidents have been occurring at various places in the country at regular intervals. In the US, on the other hand, gun culture has become an order of the day with teenagers killing their schoolmates by shooting at random in classrooms or other places. What is more dangerous in the commission of such diabolical crimes is the fact that the young people involved do not show remorse for their acts even later. On the other hand, they stick to the view that whatever they had done was normal and justified This trend, therefore, has serious ramification for the society.

Notes & References

(i) *International Law on the Rights of the child*

The Universal Declaration of Human Rights adopted by the United Nations in 1948 recognises rights of the child in various forms, like the right to life, dignity, equality, justice, etc.

In 1989, the General Assembly of the UN adopted the *Convention on the Rights of the Child.* It considered the enormous difficulties the children all over the world face. Difficulties take many forms; for example,

a. children born of poor parents do not get enough food, clothing and even shelter.

b. they have no or very little health care and nutrition.

c. they live in most unhygienic environment in company of other unlucky children.

d. many live on streets and footpaths, thus have no privacy while taking bath or answering nature's call.

e. many children are abused by adults who take opportunity of their helplessness.

f. many children are orphans while parents of some are unable to work properly ; in such cases children have to work. Unfortunately, they are paid very little in spite of working very hard and for long hours.

g. child workers are beaten and tortured by many heartless people; girl child working as a domestic servant is a worst sufferer of many kinds of abuse, including sexual abuse.

h. children are kidnapped and sold for many purposes, like begging , prostitution, etc .

i. children are *discriminated against* , that is treated unjustly, on the ground of colour, race, caste, language, religion, property, physical disability, status of birth, social origin, etc; many are denied the facility of basic education.

j. *in conflict zones* (that is, at places where armed fighting takes place), children face the worst of nightmares because they are more or less made the cannon fodder. They are used as child soldiers as was being done by the LTTE in Sri Lanka; elsewhere when families become victims of terror attacks, the children also die violent death; or if they survive, their sufferings know no bounds.

k. children have a basic right to education, which is denied to them if they are born of poor parents; they cannot bear the expenses of schooling and on the other hand, they have to go to work if they want to survive.

l. children take to drug abuse out of frustration or being forced by *traffickers*.

The Convention on the Rights of the Child has laid down the following principles, namely,

- to ensure equality (and abolish discrimination),
- to promote the best interests of the child,
- governments to protect the rights of the child,

- parents should do their duties to the child,
- all concerned to respect the views of the child,

(ii) It is not possible to entirely stop 'child labour' in this country, since the economic condition of thousands of families here is so bad that children belonging to them have no choice but to go for work; otherwise, they will simply starve.

(iii) *The Times of India*, October, 7, 2007.

Chapter - XVII

Care for Children

In ordinary life, families do not give much importance on the feelings of a child except what normal affection calls for. The normal belief is that the child has to grow up as per wishes of the parents. The society expects the child to be seen in good health and doing well in studies, sports, etc and if there comes some difficult problem in the normal growth of the child, it is just taken as bad luck. Parents and guardians are generally oblivious, if not totally ignorant, of the need for a careful sustenance of the child's mental development by carefully observing the emotional turmoil, if any, being suffered by the child. Indifference to the child's emotional problems may lead to serious behavioural abnormalities, which may gradually tend to deteriorate over a period of time. Thus comes to the fore *a problem child.*

Causes of behavioural disorder

There could be many psychological and physical reasons responsible for the problems of a problem child. The psychological reasons could be

- broken home,
- parents having no time to be with the child owing to occupational or other reasons,
- lack of sexual morality of either or both the parents,
- exposure to too much of wealth,
- sibling rivalry,
- perceived partisan behaviour of either of or both the parents/teachers,
- physical beating by parents, guardians and teachers,
- humiliation inflicted on the child publicly or privately leading to loss of its self-esteem,

- company of criminal relatives or neighbours or friends,
- falling for or picking up the habit of taking alcohol or drugs,
- family's value system and its disciplinary practices, etc.

At the early stages of life, behavioural disorder in a child gets expression in habits like thumb sucking, nail-biting, head banging, rocking movement of the body, enuresis (bed wetting), stammering, etc. Once such disorders are noticed, professional help from a psychiatrist trained in child psychiatry is called for. It may be mentioned here that even adult problems like sudden changes in mood, anxiety neurosis, sleeplessness, etc may also find way to a child's disposition when the problem becomes acute with the former. Disorder in a child's behaviour is normally accompanied by its lack of social interaction and difficulty in communication. Among the physical reasons quoted for behavioural disorder in children, the role of age, gender, malnutrition, anaemia, a debilitating ailment, pre-natal problems, infection, etc. is considered very important. The incidence of such disorder among the children in our country is very high, almost to the order of 21 per cent.

Its management

The management of behaviour disorder in children is a delicate task. While the application of appropriate medicinal treatment could be one of the ways to handle the situation, it has to be more of a psychological approach. Here comes the role of the parents/ guardians, the teachers and the society at large. A good school teacher through his (or her) efforts can control the child's total behaviour which encompasses aggression, non-compliance, attention problems, impulsivity, truancy, hyperactivity and delinquency. He (or she) can also help the child overcome its anxiety, fear, shyness, low self-esteem, sadness and depression. The part to be played by parents in the above is both primary and complementary. In other words, they go parallel. Moreover, it has to be realised by all parents that there should be adequate preparation for parenthood for each and every child before it is born.

Genetic problems

Children sometimes are afflicted by genetic problems. The following case study illustrates the problem in its true perspective:

Right from the beginning, the attitudinal problems of his 14-year-old son Anisur did not escape Sadiur Rehman's attention. The boy would otherwise pick up fights with almost every body at home, at school and everywhere else. Sadiur, a brick-trader near Diamond Harbour, 60-km away from Calcutta, took the conduct of his son as 'adolescent unruliness', which, he thought, would fade away as he would grow up.

As days went by, things, however, took a turn for the worse. Anisur would now fly into rage for no reason, attack even his kid sisters most recklessly; utter words incoherently while saliva would drool off his mouth. Elders advised Sadiur to call in an exorcist but being a Science graduate, he now understood that the boy had developed some problem in the brain. Taken to a doctor, the boy was given some anti-psychotic drugs but it did not show any improvement. He became very weak and developed frightening convulsions and tremors. Finally, he was taken to the Bangur Institute of Neurology at the SSKM Hospital, Kolkata. The neurologist at the hospital diagnosed the ailment as a notorious hereditary disorder called *Wilson's disease*. During tests it was found that the boy had a brown ring in the cornea and his blood and urine had a high level of copper, which got accumulated in his eyes, brain, kidneys and liver. With the correct treatment given, Anisur showed gradual improvement.

Wilson's disease remains largely unrecognised in this country. Approximately, one out of 30,000 people may suffer from this genetic disorder. Says Dr Kunal Roy of Indian Institute of Chemical Biology, Jadavpur, 'the worrisome fact is that one out 90 people unwittingly act as a carrier of the abnormal gene, which may be inherited from the father or the mother and accentuated by copper deposits in some parts of the body.

[Ref Silent Epidemic, Knowhow, The Telegraph, dated. 3. 10. 2005]

Juvenile delinquency

Children in their teens have a strong tendency to rebel unreasonably against anything that they come across. That is because adolescence is a period when they tend to become frustrated, confused, stressed and even lonely. This is the time the acts of juveniles get characterised by behaviourial disorder. In other words, their behaviour comes to have anti-social content like wrongful disobedience, temperamental fighting, stealing, lying, destructive attitude, cruelty to animals, vandalism, sexual misdemeanour, drug abuse, addiction to pornography, cyber crime, etc. Sometimes such behaviour escalates to the area of criminal offences punishable in law.

Causes

a. ***Genetic factors:*** Some studies indicate that chromosomal abnormality or glandular imbalance may be at the bottom of juvenile delinquency because they affect the total personality of the juvenile.

b. ***Organic factors:*** Brain dysfunction or mental retardation may be a factor in inducing delinquent behaviour during adolescence.

c. ***Environmental factors:*** Unfavourable environment has an extremely negative impact on the personality of a child. This gradually contributes to the building up of delinquency in the child's behaviour pattern. Initial delinquency of negligible nature thereafter turns into an irresistible criminal attitude and conduct too deep-seated to be corrected. The origin of the said factors is found in the family, in the society and in the peer group to which the child belongs:

In the family

- Ignorance about childcare.
- Too rigid discipline or lack of it.
- Uncared for childhood.
- The child viewing immoral and dishonest conduct in the family.
- Corruption and unethical business practices by parents and elders.
- Persistent conflict among the members and torture of women in the family.
- Broken home/cruelty of step-mother/divorced parents.
- Alcoholism in the family.
- Hurting of self-esteem of the child by constant criticism/ beating/scolding and undeserved punishment.
- Availability to the child of too much of money, much more than its legitimate needs.
- Indulgence to the child even in its patently wrong conduct.

- Lack of leisure hours owing to over-emphasis on study.
- Higher level of education compared to the child's ability.

In the society

- Lack of recreational facilities in the vicinity.
- Lack of good schools, etc. in the locality.
- Lack of a value system in the social arena.
- Unsavoury influence of movies and the media.
- Exhibitionism.

Among the peer group

- Bad company for viewing pornography, horror movies, etc/ reading sex thrillers, cheap type of literature.
- Anti-social activity by way of extortion, eve-teasing, use of muscle power for settling scores, etc.
- Drug abuse in compact groups.

[Ref 'Behavioural Problems in Children' (2001) Indian Academy of Paediatrics, Assam Branch,]

Conclusion

When the causes of a problem are known or have been found out, the remedy should not be far to seek. The only way care can be taken of children is to make sure that the factors responsible for their delinquency are eliminated by individual, family and group action.

Researches have shown that the incidence of juvenile delinquency is higher in families of low-income groups and illiterate parents. Even in America, higher juvenile crime rates are said to be found among the Blacks, the obvious reason being their comparative economic and educational backwardness. However, delinquency develops at ease also in families belonging to the higher economic strata owing to many of the factors enumerated above.

The conventional method of dealing with juvenile delinquency is to place the offender under institutional care and to impart to him vocational and perhaps some other *remedial* education. But it has also been seen that non-institutional care, like providing *appropriate counselling*, *canalising the creative energies of the delinquent* and *addressing the causes of his aberrations,* do go a long way to solve the problem.

The print and the electronic media have a great amount of responsibility for curbing the publication/telecast of real and imaginary crime and conflict based stories in their pages and screen since the gruesome and immoral tales generally highlighted by them often inspire the young minds in taking a wrong and violent path.

Schools and other educational institutions, particularly the teachers, have to take the initiative to impart a value-based education to the child so that they grow up with a sense of values for their future. This is the best care they can take for the good of the children and the society.

Chapter - XVIII

DNA Fingerprinting

What is DNA Fingerprinting?

DNA Fingerprinting is the newest tool for modern day scientific investigation. It was invented in 1985 by scientist Sir Alec Jeffrey of Leicester University, UK and since then the method is being increasingly put to use in the investigation of cases of rape, murder, disputed paternity, identification of mutilated bodies, etc. Originally intended for investigation of sex offences, the technique was extended to varieties of clueless cases against human body. Scientists call the process 'DNA Profiling'.

DNA or deoxyriboneuclic acid is a matter found in all living bodies. It is the basic genetic material and the carrier of basic genetic traits. It carries the genetic codes that determine physical traits such as those of race, sex, hair and eye colour. It has been found that no two persons, except identical twins, have identical DNA. Another characteristic of DNA is that it can be located even in the remnants of a body long years after the person had died. Semen and blood cells are particularly rich in DNA and thus DNA fingerprinting is especially useful in solving wide-ranging crimes relating to rape and murder.

Characteristics of DNA

The DNA fingerprinting process shows the difference between individuals in the form of the sets of bands on a photographic film, something like the bar-code of a product. It has been scientifically established that a child inherits 50 per cent of the bar-codes of its mother and the remaining 50 per cent from its father. Identical twins, however, have identical bar-codes. It, therefore, follows that related individuals have higher co-efficient of similarity in respect of DNA than unrelated individuals.

Composition

DNA is made up of four chemical bases, which are like teeth in a zipper and arranged in a spiral. The chemicals, abbreviated as 'a', 'T', 'C' and 'G', are arranged in pairs – a and T are combined together as are C and G. DNA comprises billions of these bases, their combinations being unique to each person. To do a DNA test, scientists take physical evidences such as blood or semen extracts and determine the sequence of DNA bases in the said extracts. Labs commonly test in exhibits (taken from the crime scene) specific segments where bases repeat in pairs that vary from person to person. They then compare the DNA of the crime scene exhibit with that of the suspect.

Police investigation

It, therefore, follows that the police should look for sources of DNA at the crime scene to connect the victim to the crime and the criminal. Sources of DNA in incidents of assault, rape, murder, etc are minute and available in innocuous items like hair roots, blood stains, semen drops, cigarette stubs, saliva, any other body fluid (dried or otherwise), body tissues, bones, skin patches and so on.

In criminal investigation, it is the task of the investigating officer to link up the offenders (or suspects) with the crime committed by producing evidences of the latter's coming into contact with the victim. The above items minutely observed and detected at the crime scene will indicate the DNA of the offender in lab tests and if it turns out to be the same after comparison with that of the suspect, it establishes the presence of the accused or the suspect at the scene.

Picking up materials from the victim's body at the crime scene for DNA clues entails a high degree of caution and precision on the part of the IO The biggest danger is cross-contamination from other samples. The officer concerned should collect samples (exhibits) using separate gloves for each sample. Even otherwise, it needs a trained hand to collect samples of blood, semen and other body fluids from the crime scene.

[The authorities should, therefore, arrange the training of all prospective investigating officers in the art of sample collection under the supervision of forensic experts.]

For the purpose of DNA fingerprinting, a volume of 10 ml of heparinised blood is required in the case of an adult. The requirement would be of a volume of 2 to 5 ml in the case of a child. For identification of a deceased person, blood samples of his or her nearest relations like mother, father or children should be collected for comparison with the DNA materials gathered from the crime scene. Blood samples should be kept on ice in a thermos flask properly sealed and certified. Tooth, bone or hair should be packed in dry polythene bags. Seminal/vaginal swab should be placed in a clean dried glass vial (bottle) and sealed. Muscle tissues close to the bone should be dissected and about 100 grams of tissues should be sent in a glass bottle. Bloodstains should be sent in a dried polythene bag properly sealed.

DNA fingerprinting is a complex scientific process and entails a lot of scientist's time and energy. It is inordinately expensive. Only a few forensic science institutes in India have the facilities for the test. It, therefore, ought to be sought only in very important cases. In this connection, even the Supreme Court has opined that DNA test should not be directed as a matter of routine.[1]

Success story of DNA Tests

Scientists unlocking the secret genetic code that makes each human unique can identify killers as well as establish innocence. In recent years, it was by application of this method that the remains of Czar Nicholas II of pre-revolution Russia could be identified. In one instance, DNA findings from the semen stains found on a famous woman's dress had threatened the reputation of a president of the United States in recent times.

Following are some of the examples of DNA fingerprinting that proved useful in the investigation of crimes:

In 1987 in England, the police investigating the rape and murder of two teen aged girls took blood samples from more than 500 people (of every man between 13 years and 30 years in three villages) and it was the genetic material of one Colin Pitchfork that matched the semen recovered from the bodies of the deceased. This led to the arrest of the culprit and he was convicted and given a life sentence. He thus became the first rapist-cum-murderer to be caught by DNA.[2] The story is not complete without mentioning Rodney Buckland,

---

1 Banarsi Das *vs* Teeku Dutta (2005) 4 SCC 449.

2 The case was detected in Leicester, the very place where the technique was invented only two years before.

the 17-year-old boy, who was originally suspected in one of the said murders and therefore was the first person in history to a cleared of a crime on DNA evidence.

In 1988, one Timothy Spencer was sentenced to death in Virginia (US) on the basis of DNA evidence. He was charged for multiple rapes and murder and was executed in 1994. David Vasquez, who was initially convicted of one of Spencer's crimes, was exonerated on the basis of the same DNA profile.

In another case in Andhra Pradesh, a person was strangulated to death by the intruder who, unfortunately for himself, left a bit of his finger in the mouth of the murdered person. The DNA of the finger remnant bitten off by the deceased matched with that of a suspect and he was arrested.

In the Rajiv Gandhi assassination case in 1991, investigators had two problems to contend with, namely, to establish the identity of the body of Rajiv Gandhi and to establish the fact that the human bomb Dhanu had indeed put a bomb on her body with a Denim belt on her waist. Both the problems got solved by DNA fingerprinting. By computerized DNA-fingerprinting, it was established that the Denim belt, which held the bomb, was indeed worn by Dhanu.

In the well-known 'Lakshmi vs Mary case' (two names for the same five-year-old girl), Lakshmi, a daughter of a gypsy couple, was claimed by another couple that had lost their daughter Mary. The latter couple claimed that the girl was not Lakshmi but Mary. The case was investigated by application of DNA fingerprinting on the child and the claimant couples. The girl turned out to be the child of the gypsy couple.

In 1992, a civil engineer in Hyderabad was told by his doctor that he was infertile because his sperm count was low. The doctor apparently was not aware that such a condition did not preclude the ability of the semen to fertilize. As the engineer already had two children, he suspected adultery by his wife and filed a petition for divorce. DNA test established to his joy and embarrassment that he was indeed the father of his two children.

DNA fingerprinting also prevents women from getting away with adultery. In Kare district in 1993, Rajashree (name changed) had a child by her paramour but she insisted that the child was her husband's. In the litigation that followed, DNA fingerprinting established that the child wasn't from her husband. He thus got divorce from his wife without having to pay alimony.

Legal aspects

DNA fingerprinting has some inherent infirmities also. This high-level precision technology has not yet been formally recognised in the Indian Evidence Act.

Section 53 CrPC, which allows even forcible medical examination of an arrested person does not specifically authorise a police officer to collect blood sample from an accused person for DNA test without his consent.

Recently, in a case of gang rape of a student of Maulana Abul Kalam Azad Medical College in Delhi on December 24, 2002, doctors at the Safdar Jung Hospital took the prime accused Rahul's blood sample following a court order to that effect. In the sensational murder case of poetess Madhumita in UP, the accused Amarmani Tripathy was also ordered to undergo DNA test. In both the cases, the involvement of the accused in the related crimes got proved, thanks to the test results.

In case of refusal by the accused to the taking of his blood for DNA test despite there being a court order to that effect, the court will be free to draw an adverse inference against the accused.

However, there are chances of pitfalls in the use of the technique of DNA fingerprinting for justice delivery in criminal cases. The court should take care about the sources of materials used for DNA profiling and satisfy itself that the procedures laid down for obtaining the profile were meticulously followed by the police and the forensic scientists concerned. The investigating officer also need be careful about the possibility of the criminal himself planting fake DNA materials in the crime scene to mislead investigation. In one case, a criminal had even planted fake DNA evidence on his own body to implicate his opponent.

Creation of database

The technology of DNA fingerprinting has a vast scope for organising data bases of various tribes, communities, races, etc and to that extent has usefulness for wide-ranging scientific studies. But the greatest drawback of this technology is that it can be put to use maliciously against certain communities and races for ulterior purposes. One shudders to think what Hitler would have done had this technology been available to him in the early years of the 20th century.

The utility of DNA fingerprinting in combating crimes has been recognised all over the world. The nation states can build up their DNA database of all persons convicted or suspected in criminal cases so that suspects in unsolved crimes can be traced from the list of criminals already on record. This will have ample justification since it has been seen that many a person tends to repeat the crime, which he has already committed once.

DNA databases are generally government-controlled. The United States has the largest DNA database, holding over 5 million records of individuals (as of 2007). It is expanding with every passing day.

The UK has its 'National DNA Data Base' (NDNAD) of a similar size. It was established following a decision of the British Government to make DNA tests compulsory for criminals. The objective of the creation of this database, as the then British Prime Minister Tony Blair had said in 1999, would be to store 'genetic fingerprints' of all known criminals on computer so as to make the drive against crimes easier. The job was entrusted to the police though civil liberty groups resented the decision. The implication of this decision is that anyone who is involved in a crime and arrested comes on the database. Then when a fresh crime is committed, the police could go into it and see if the DNA at the scene of the crime matched with the DNA of the suspect.[1]

In England and Wales, any arrested suspect must submit DNA sample for storage. In Scotland, DNA profiles of persons acquitted have to be removed from the database. In Sweden, convicts serving two years or more shall have profiles in the database. France and New Zealand, among other western nations, have their own databases. Originally intended for sex offenders, databases have gradually been created for criminals of all types.

Endnotes

1. There has now come some court intervention in the process of the maintenance of a DNA database in Britain. The European Human Rights Court in Strasbourg (France) ruled on December 4, 2008 that the British Government had violated the privacy of some persons by storing their DNA profile. The ruling centered on a boy (aged 11 years)

who was charged with attempted robbery and a man who was charged with harassing his partner before the case was formally discontinued. Both of them had applied for destruction of their fingerprints, DNA samples and profiles but the police refused to do so on the basis of an existent law. It was argued on behalf of the aggrieved persons that it cast suspicion on them despite their acquittal. The court felt that such an act 'failed to strike a balance between competing public and private interests'.

2. The Police, however, defended their right to retain DNA profiles on the ground that it had helped the identification of many criminals. "From May 2001 to December 2005, 2,00,000 DNA samples were retained on the National DNA Database, which would previously have had to be removed as they were taken from people charged but not convicted of offences. Of these, about 8,500 profiles of individuals have been linked with crime scenes involving nearly 14,000 offences. (The Times of India, December 6, 2008)

Chapter - XIX

Communal Violence

Eruption of violence (and the resultant disruption of public order) that may follow a gradual build-up of tension between two communities in a given area is known as a 'communal riot'. It might as well be sparked off all of a sudden by a freak incident, which could not have been anticipated. The word 'communal' has acquired a distinct connotation in India over the years to mean something quite different from what it perhaps conveys in the rest of the English-speaking world. The word is an adjective relating to the noun 'commune' (or 'community') and therefore it is supposed to be used to relate to or describe something when a community as a whole is involved in a matter, not necessarily as adversaries against another community. However, in India, it has come to signify a hostile situation obtaining for the time being between two communities opposed to each other on a certain issue. Thus when we use the expression 'communal tension',[1] it presupposes the existence of an adversarial relationship between two communities. In our common understanding, it tends to mean a tense relationship between the communities involved.

Characteristics of a communal riot

A communal riot in India is usually a conflict situation – involving active hostilities - between two major religious communities.[2] It

---

1 Communal tension can be defined as a situation that is associated with group hatred, a sense of fear and an aggressive disposition on the part of the communities concerned. In other words, it is an animated state of antagonism – a 'stand-off' - with the possibility of an outbreak of violence anytime soon.

2 The 2002 Gujarat riots are a classic example of a Hindu-Muslim communal riot in recent times. It got sparked off by the killing at

Contd...

is invariably accompanied with a very high degree of ferocity and destructive ethos against both human lives and properties. Even cattle and other livestock are not spared. In legal terms, a 'riot' is a conflict between five or more persons, where criminal force is used by members of 'an unlawful assembly' upon one another, leading generally to spilling of blood, and perhaps even death, of one or more individuals and concomitant destruction of properties of the adversaries. Targeted killings of innocent men, women and children and random arson are necessary accompaniments of such a riot. Rape of women, regardless of their age, is also very common in communal riots. Weapons ranging from primitive instruments like knives, swords, spears, hatchets, etc. to firearms and explosives are freely used to wreak vengeance upon persons with whom the rioters otherwise have no personal enmity.

A communal riot can be of such a dimension and intensity that it may result in the butchering of thousands of persons belonging to the communities involved, over rather a short period of time, ranging from a few hours to a few days, before it is brought under control. In such an event, destruction of public and private properties runs into crores of rupees. The frenzy that overtakes the society in such a situation defies any rational explanation. What is more distressing is that mistrust and hatred that get generated between the affected communities in a given area, where such a riot has taken place, persist for years. Dithering by the authorities from taking firm action well in time to thwart the conflict contributes to its escalation like bushfire.

One of the important aspects of communal riots in India is that the minority community always ends up having a higher percentage of victims, no matter who had started the conflict. In many cases, it is simply a one-sided aggression, with the victims hardly willing or being able to retaliate.

Communal Riots in India

Before we examine the role of the police in preventing and quelling communal riots, we shall briefly go into its history in India.

Contd... Godhra (Gujarat) of 59 Hindu *Karsewaks* (religious volunteers)) by an act of arson on the train compartment by which they were traveling back home from Ayodhya. The arsonists were suspectedly some Muslim vendors of Godhra Railway Station. The anti-Christian riots in Orissa in 2008 also had the colour of a communal riot.

Muslim rule in India had its beginning with the Arab invasion of the Sind province (now in Pakistan) in 10th century AD. Different dynasties of Muslim rulers have since ruled in different parts of the country till the British overthrew them step-by-step in the 18th century. However, recorded history does not indicate the occurrence of any communal riot of the kind we witness in modern India. The origin of communal riots in the form we see now can be traced back to the beginning of the 20th century when the authority of the British started being challenged by Indians for the first time. With the expansion of modern education primarily in the 19th century, Indians started aspiring to throw off the yoke of foreign rule and the confrontation that followed unnerved the British rulers. They now felt that they must devise a way to divide the Indian society on religious line so that they could continue as the arbiter of our destiny.

After the Sepoy Mutiny in 1857, the British government pursued a conscious policy of keeping the Muslim elite away from positions of power but when the Indian National Congress, having been born in 1885, started challenging the authority of the British, they thought it was time the Muslims were put up on a separate forum as rivals to the Congress. The Swadeshi Movement, following the partition of Bengal by Lord Curzon in 1905, further gave a fillip to their resolve. They, therefore, encouraged the formation of the Muslim League[3] in the first decade of the 20th century, thus sowing the first seed of a permanent Hindu-Muslim divide on a confrontational line. The later movements of the Congress, therefore, found rival Muslim movements vitiating the relationship between the two major communities.[4] The 'Communal Award' announced by the British government in the 1930s for separate electorates for Hindus and Muslims embittered the inter-community relations, deepening the mistrust for each other. Mistrust later started degenerating into hatred for each other. The climax was reached with MA Jinnah's Muslim League passing the Pakistan Resolution in 1940, demanding a separate homeland for the Muslims to be created by dividing the country. Hindus never took this kindly.

Communal riots - of both small and big dimensions - had been taking place in different cities, rural areas and *mahallas* in undivided

---

3 The Muslim League was formed in Dacca (now Dhaka) in 1906.

4 Mahatma Gandhi, however, tried to dissipate the developing antagonism between Hindus and Muslims at this critical juncture of history.

India along with the aforesaid political developments. As the Second World War took a virulent turn by 1941, the British in India became increasingly desperate[5]. With the Congress starting the Quit India Movement (and top Congress leaders, including Mahatma Gandhi, being put under indefinite detention) in 1942, it became a field day for Jinnah to convert the inter-community hatred into fury and madness. At the end of the war, a British Cabinet Mission came to India (in 1946) offering a good number of concessions to Jinnah raising hopes that 'partition' of the country would mercifully be averted but the Muslim League would have none of it short of the creation of Pakistan.[6] Jinnah, with a view to pushing his demand for 'Pakistan' to a point of no return, declared the 16th Day of August 1946 as the 'Direct Action Day'. Consequently, Calcutta saw for the next three days butchery and arson of an unprecedented scale. During the ongoing conflict and savagery, the Hindus were at the receiving end while the provincial government of Bengal under Sahid Shurawardy (who later became Prime Minister of Pakistan) abdicated their duties entirely and encouraged the 'Leaguers' to carry on with the mayhem. Significantly, the British Governor of Bengal, gullible as he was, allowed himself to be lulled into what Shurawardy had to tell him. In the face of this situation, Hindus and Sikhs of this great city organised themselves in their own way and came down on to the streets of both Calcutta and Howrah to retaliate with a near equal ferocity. 'The Great Calcutta Killing,' as it is known, now infamously became 'the mother of all communal riots' in British India. A minimum of five thousand lives was lost in the twin city in just a matter of three days.[7] The divide created by this spread of hatred and blood-letting never got completely healed up till today.

Following the Great Calcutta Killing, it was clear to the British Government as well as the Indian leaders that the country had to be partitioned even as freedom came, to avoid a civil war. Thus,

---

5 The Government needed co-operation of Indians for mobilising resources for the war effort.

6 It was not that the League rejected the Cabinet mission offer entirely because of the intransigence of MA Jinnah. Congress leaders, including Pandit Jawaharlal Nehru, also made some flip-flop that finally led to a fiasco and the partition of the country.

7 Leonard Mosley, The Last Days of the British Raj, (1966), Jaico Publishing House, Bombay.

Pakistan was born in 1947 simultaneously with the advent of India's independence. However, the vivisection of the country did not take away the communal virus. Killing, destruction of properties and the consequent migration of both the communities (including Sikhs) that followed were of a scale unknown in history. It took a couple of years for things to settle down.

In independent India, however, we never got rid of the problem entirely during the last six decades since 1947. Very many places have seen communal riots of the nature experienced during the pre-independence days. Among the places where such riots have occurred more than once are Ahmedabad, Mumbai, Meerat, Calcutta, Aligarh, Moradabad, Surat, Bhagalpur and Hyderabad, to name a few places. There are innumerable places where communal riots have occurred in a smaller scale also. Many a time, a communal riot that ensues at a certain place escalates swiftly to engulf an entire state or even a couple of states. Post Babri Masjid riots in December 1992 and post Godhra riots in 2002 were of the latter type. Post-independence India has also seen communal riots of huge dimensions against religious communities other than Muslims, for example the anti-Sikh riots of 1984 (in Delhi and other places) and anti-Christian riots of 2008 (in Orissa). Major riots have always taken a heavy toll in terms of hundreds, and sometime thousands, of lives and hundreds of crores worth of properties. It has, therefore, become one of our pre-occupations to cater for a regular arrangement to contain communal riots in every state and district in the country.

Factors causing communal tension/riots

It is essential that the police and the administration have a theoretical background of the causes that lead to eruption of communal violence in the country. Countless numbers of enquiries, including those by Commissions of Enquiry, have been held at different points of time to identify the reasons behind such riots and come to conclusions. Studies, however, have shown that such riots get triggered by various individual factors, or a combination of factors, many a time on extremely flimsy grounds.

The following can be cited as very common causes of communal riots in India, now that the British are no longer in picture:

1. Religious or even socio-religious procession of a community passing by a place of worship of the other; clashes commence with taunts, brick-batting etc.

2. Entry of a pig into a Muslim area or a place of worship.
3. Slaughter of a cow at a public place or a private place visible to the public or even a rumour to that effect.
4. Kidnapping or even consensual marriage of a woman from one community by a member of the other.
5. Murder of or attack on a person belonging to one community by a member of the other.
6. Dispute over a plot of land.[8]
7. Snide remarks considered offensive to a community.
8. Spraying of 'colour' during the Holi festival.
9. Rumours or reports of some atrocity elsewhere on members of a particular community.
10. Eve-teasing of a girl from a particular community by young men from another community.
11. Desecration of a temple, or a mosque, or a mausoleum, or a graveyard (*e.g.* the incident of throwing of eggs on a Ganesh temple that happened in Pune in 2008).
12. A political assassination can trigger a riot against a community (*e.g.* anti-Sikh riots in 1984 following the assassination of Indira Gandhi).[9]
13. Resentment generating from alleged religious conversion (*e.g.* anti-Christian riots in 2008 in Orissa. Certain tribal areas in Gujarat had also seen anti-Christian riots on this ground a couple of years back.).
14. Terrorists always stand to gain from a communal riot. Many a time they start the mayhem and others follow the lead (*e.g.* the random killing of Hindi-speaking labourers in various parts of Assam in November 2003 and later).
15. Holding of Friday prayers or a Puja on a busy road blocking the movement of traffic or pedestrians (*e.g.* at Tiljala near Park Circus in Kolkata).
16. Miscellaneous causes.

---

8 The communal riots in Udalguri and Darrang districts of Assam in late 2008 owe their origin to the resentment of the local tribal communities for the loss of their cultivable land to encroachers suspected to be Bangladeshi immigrants. Violence erupted here in a big way with just an isolated incident of assault.

9 The 2008 Orissa riots against Christians also got sparked off by the assassination of a Swamiji.

The above list is not exhaustive but only shows how a communal riot can start even with an insignificant spark. Politicians of different hues and levels almost invariably add to the escalation of the situation in a big way by their overt and covert activities. They take a confusing situation such as this as an opportunity to expand their political base and influence, regardless of the pain and misery a communal riot brings upon their own people.

An all-India Fact sheet [10]

Year	Number of cases
2000	599
2001	824
2002	722
2003	711
2004	677
2005	779
2006	698
2007	761
2008	943

According to a paper circulated at a meeting of the National Integration Council held in October 2008,[11] India had 6,464 incidents of communal violence from the year 2000 to September 2008. While 2,393 people were killed, about 21,077 people were injured in these violent incidents.

Role of the Police

A communal riot is a challenging proposition for the police. Here, they must exert themselves properly and adequately to meet the situation with equanimity, a sense of fairness and a balanced judgement. It is not a simple law and order problem to be attended to in so far as the fall-out of a communal riot has wide-ranging ramifications. The common methods adopted by the police in ordinary law and order situations are almost always inadequate for handling a communal riot, which needs a much greater degree of circumspection to deal with.

10 Statement of the MoS, Home, in Rajya Sabha on December 9, 2009.

11 The Times of India, October.15, 2008.

Hence, the magistracy and the police should work as a close-knit team right from the beginning and their approach should be one of firm action, and not of dithering. Strong measures to nip a developing situation in the bud should be taken by the authorities right on sighting the first spark – it has been found to be the easiest way to control a communal flare-up. It is for this reason that state governments keep the DM and the SP personally responsible for controlling communal riots in their respective jurisdictions. This has been the national administrative policy since the mid-1960s. Pre-emptive actions to thwart a communal flare-up have always paid dividends. As our countrywide experience shows, dithering on the part of the DM or the SP has always resulted in greater loss of life and property.

Some distinctive measures that have an immense bearing on the efforts of the police to contain a communal riot are noted below:

Sensitivity to the situation – The police down to the SHO level should have a high degree of sensitivity to the prevailing relationship between different communities in a given jurisdiction. They should have a police station level channel of advance information to keep themselves abreast of developments and to help communities concerned foster a healthy relationship. This is the best way to avert communal tension and a flare-up. Hence, the SHO should be asked to create and maintain a network of intelligence in his area of responsibility without dependence on the State Intelligence Branch[12] If worked on properly, the information system of the SHO will never let him down.

Action plan – In many cases it has been found that the police fail to react to a developing situation on time and get overwhelmed in confusion when a communal riot breaks out unexpectedly. This is because they, to begin with, did not have an action plan to work on. A "contingency' action plan is therefore a 'must' for the police as a measure of preparedness for a communal riot. It should be updated at least once in three months on the basis of fresh inputs received and the changing resource position at their command.

Essentially such an action plan should be there at the district level, with provision for extra resources to be deployed quickly in sensitive areas. The police station should keep up-to-date all its records relating to anti-social elements, minority pockets, and communication layout

12 Many a time the State Intelligence Branch is taken unawares by developments on the communal front.

including road conditions within and without. A promptly responsive communication system, a good and imaginative deployment of force, posting of impartial officers in sensitive police stations, a good reserve of force and vehicles, an unambiguous set of instructions for the cutting edge level of officers and the fixing of supervisory roles for senior police officers are some of the ingredients of a good action plan for the purpose.

Organising Preventive Measures – The District SP should put into effect the action plan at the first sign of a communal trouble. All known and potential trouble-makers should be booked under the preventive provisions of law. These measures take away the driving force of the trouble-shooters and make them destitutes in the field. Thus, the situation is saved.

Inter-community dialogue – In the face of a communal situation, the police, together with the DM, must try to bring together opinion leaders of the communities involved and sort out the issues of contention by application of goodwill and when necessary, with a bit of coercion. Such dialogues have been found very useful in umpteen numbers of cases in defusing adverse situations and should be used as a tool by the administration in maintaining law and order.

Pre-emptive use of force – While mediatory persuasions continue, the police should not be averse to making pre-emptive use of force where necessary to exhibit their determination to stop the trouble at any cost. This, however, will require the best of judgement of the situation and the police must carry the DM along.

Care for evacuees – A communal riot invariably throws up evacuees, the number of whom is determined by its intensity and expanse. They remain panicky and tend to react to even small provocations and simple rumours most unreasonably and disproportionately. They, therefore, remain a source of further spread and intensification of the flare-up that had already occurred. The police should discharge a special responsibility towards the evacuees by showing them empathy and creating confidence in their mind by their actions. The police should try to help them by taking meticulous care in each individual case of distress.

This may be done in many ways, for example, (i) by helping out the medical treatment of the evacuee's family members who might have sustained serious injuries during the riot, or (ii) by helping locate his missing family members and retrieve his lost properties, or (iii) by arranging the restoration of landed property of which he had perhaps been dispossessed. Extension of the help has to be imaginative and spontaneous.

The part played by the police in helping persons in distress to overcome their trauma goes a long way to defuse a riotous situation. It does not cost the police anything much beyond a measure of energy but the result it gives makes it worthwhile.

Prompt and Unbiased Investigation/Prosecution of Riot Cases – A communal riot leaves in its trail mountains of grievances against the wrong-doers. Such a riot gives an opportunity to criminals and communalists to further their cause. They have no scruple in inflicting untold sorrows on its victims. It shakes the people's confidence in the state and its law-enforcing machinery. It is, therefore, the duty of the police to investigate the crimes promptly and impartially and prosecute the offenders. Delay in bringing the wrong-doers to book keeps the seed of communal tension alive and the victims would naturally keep waiting seeking an opportunity to avenge themselves.

Bottom-line

We have yet to find a permanent remedy to the communal problem in this country. Time and again it raises its ugly head and overwhelms the body politic. It is both a political and a social problem. However, till such time it gets eradicated, we should keep our powder dry. We should not prove ourselves to be a soft state. We should act firmly whenever it is necessary. Long-term remedy to this old problem, however, lies in a sustained social, economic and educational development of all the communities.

Chapter - XX

FAQ
(Frequently Asked Questions with Answers)

It has commonly been seen that many officers at the cutting edge level get confused as to what they should do under certain circumstances in the course of performing their duties. They face predicament while confronting some peculiar situations but do not find to have had readymade answers for such situations. Effort has been made in this Chapter to deal with questions in such situations:

1. The police are empowered under Section 41 of CrPC to arrest a person on mere suspicion. Do they have to justify such arrest?

Suspicion as a ground for arrest cannot be entirely subjective. It must be 'reasonable' in the given circumstances. Such an arrest may be effected only with a view to prosecuting the arrestee later for taking part in the commission of a cognizable offence. The policeman concerned should assess the conduct of the arrestee prior to such arrest and be convinced that it was reasonable to suspect the latter's involvement in the offence. If the arrest cannot be properly explained, the officer will be liable for wrongfully detaining the victim (Section 342 IPC) and may also be sued in a civil court for compensation.

2. The police have the power to arrest a person under 151 CrPC to prevent him from committing a cognizable offence. What procedure should be followed after such an arrest?

This is an inherent power of the police. However, after effecting such an arrest, the police should file a report under Section 107 CrPC before an Executive Magistrate to bind the arrestee with a bond, so that he does not attempt further to make a breach of the peace.

3. The law reposes a high degree of confidence on the testimony of a rape victim, who is naturally the first witness in the prosecution of such a case. The Supreme Court has even averred that her testimony alone may be enough to convict the accused for the crime. How should the police deal with the victim in such a case?

The investigating officer and all others concerned should take extra-ordinary care in dealing with a rape victim. She should be asked questions about the occurrence with utmost care for her sensitivity and modesty. This is to be done in presence of a female relative or friend of her's. Her statement narrating the commission of the crime should be recorded first under Section 161 CrPC by the IO and then under Section 164 CrPC by a Judicial Magistrate. The latter statement should form a part of the Case Diary. The statements have to be 'in the first person'.

The place of occurrence and the clothes of both the victim and the accused should be minutely examined by the IO for DNA materials. Similarly, both should be examined in person by an authorized medical officer or a medical board, as the case may be, for detection of injuries, DNA materials, etc. to reinforce evidence in the crime. The medical officer should be requested in writing to preserve the vaginal swab of the victim for DNA fingerprinting.

4. Can a police officer call up any person to appear before him at a police station to give testimony in a criminal case he has been investigating?

Yes and No, both. Yes, he can issue an order in writing to a male person above the age of 15 years to appear at the PS in connection with an investigation.

No, he cannot do so in respect of a woman or a child below 15 years of age. In the latter case, the IO will have to go to the residence of the person concerned to examine her or him. [Section 160 CrPC]

5. What precautions should an IO take during the conduct of search of a given house or place?

A police officer conducting an investigation is authorized to carry out search of a house or place when he is of the opinion that a particular thing or things related to the commission of the concerned offence could be found there if an immediate search is made. [Section 165 CrPC] However, while conducting the search, the IO must invite some respectable persons of the locality to witness the search. And before the actual work of search commences, the IO must get himself searched by the witnesses, so that there is no suspicion, or even a plea later by the affected party, that the items found and seized during the search were indeed planted by the police officer himself.

6. What is the latest legal position regarding statutory enquiries into custodial death or rape?

The legal provisions in this respect [Section 176 (1-A) CrPC] have been fundamentally changed by the CrPC (Amendment) Act 2005.

Besides the statutory inquest by an Executive Magistrate in case of a death in the custody of the police or any other investigative agency (section 174 CrPC), it has now been laid down that there shall be a judicial enquiry in the case of death or disappearance of a person from such custody. A judicial enquiry is also compulsory in case of alleged custodial rape of a woman. The enquiry will have to be conducted by a Judicial Magistrate or a Metropolitan Magistrate, as the case may be. In such a situation, the officer-in-charge of the police station or jail concerned must keep the place of occurrence of the crime undisturbed.

7. What are the Central Government agencies involved in various types of investigation?

Criminal investigation falls in the State list under the Seventh Schedule of the Constitution. Hence the basic investigative powers are with the State Police. However, the following agencies of the Central Government are also there in the field of investigation in some special but limited areas:

The Delhi Special Police Establishment (DSPE) was originally created in 1941 to deal with the huge volumes of corruption cases in India that resulted from boundless war expenditures during the World War II (1939-45). Later, the Special Police Establishment Act 1946 gave the organisation a legal format. In 1963, the agency took the present shape and came to be known as the Central Bureau of Investigation (CBI). It reports to the Prime Minister through the Department of Personnel. Its main brief is to investigate corruption cases relating to the Union of India. However, owing to the heavy and frequent demand on the agency - as an 'impartial' body - to take over investigation of difficult and controversial criminal cases in the States, the CBI has now opened a special crimes division, which deals with the said category of cases when asked for. However, it cannot, on its own, record an FIR and investigate general cases, however sensational they might be, except with the consent or request of the State Government concerned or on the orders of a High Court or the Supreme Court of India. Like all other police agencies, it has had many successes and failures at the same time.

The National Investigation Agency (NIA) is a comparatively new creation. It came into being following the passing of the NIA Act 2008 in Parliament. In view of the tremendous escalation, in recent years, of terrorist and secessionist activities in the country, especially those in the North East and the Maoist corridor spread all over mainland India, the Central Government decided to form a specialised agency for investigation of the crimes related to such activities. Thus, the NIA has taken a good deal of burden off the CBI's table. The agency reports to the Ministry of Home Affairs.

The Enforcement Directorate (ED), controlled by the Ministry of Finance, is authorised to investigate cases under the Foreign Exchange Management Act 1999 and the Prevention of Money-Laundering Act 2002. It is tasked to go into the violation of the foreign exchange regulations.

The Directorate of Revenue Intelligence (DRI), also under the Ministry of Finance, investigates illicit-smuggling of gold and other valuable things, including international trafficking of drugs, etc.

The Narcotics Control Bureau (NCB) is an agency for enforcement of the Narcotic Drugs and Psychotropic Substances Act 1985. Here there is another agency called Central Bureau of Narcotics (CBN), which supervises the licit production of opium in central India for pharmaceutical purposes and takes up cases for violation of the Rules laid down for such production, harvesting and sale of the produce. The CBN is headed by the Narcotics Commissioner of India based at Gwalior.[1] Both the agencies are under the Ministry of Finance.

The Customs department also conducts its own investigations into suspected or real cases of the smuggling of goods – goods carried without payment of duties or which are contraband - across the international borders.

---

1 The government-sponsored production of opium for pharmaceutical purposes is done in the contiguous districts of MP, UP and Rajasthan. This is meant for manufacture of pain-relieving medicines, like Morphine, for terminal cancer patients. The harvested opium is meant for both domestic use and export to other countries. The US is the biggest importer of pharmaceutical opium from India.

8. What are the State Government agencies available for criminal investigation?

The state police are the main agency available in a State for criminal investigation. Apart from the police-station-based investigative set up, it has a number of specialised branches at the state level, like the Criminal Investigation Department (CID) or Crime Branch for difficult cases, the Anti-corruption Branch (ACB) for corruption cases, Economic Offences Branch for economic offences, etc.

Second, the State Excise department has also got some power in the investigation of cases related to liquor, narcotics, prohibition, etc.

Third, the Forest department has powers of investigation on cases related to the violation of the Indian Forest Act 1927, the Wildlife Act 1972, and other environment-related matters.

However, the police in the State have concurrent powers in almost all the subjects, which are generally under the control of other departments.

9. What legal action can be taken against the bouncing of a cheque?

The drawing of a cheque that bounces is punishable under Section 138 of the Negotiable Instruments Act 1881. As per the later amendments in the Act, the drawer of the bounced cheque could be awarded imprisonment up to two years and a fine that could be double the amount of the cheque drawn. However, the payee must file a complaint before a court to this effect after giving due notice to the drawer.

10. What is the procedure for arrest of a juvenile offender in a cognizable offence?

A 'juvenile' is a person under the age of eighteen years and is a 'child' in the eye of law. Under the Juvenile Justice (Care and Protection of Children) Act 2000, a child never commits a crime, but could be 'in conflict with law'. In such a case, if the police officer concerned thinks that the child need be detained pending further investigation for involvement in a serious offence, he may do so but shall forthwith produce him or her before the Juvenile Justice Board concerned for further orders. In case of a serious incident, when the

JJ Board orders the child's detention, he or she has to be kept in an 'Observation Home', and never in police or jail custody. The Observation Home has to be one administered or approved by the Department of Social Welfare of the state government.

11. What is the concept of 'cross-cases'? What are their uses?

When a breach of peace occurs owing to the aggressive behaviour or acts of two opposite parties in a dispute, the task of the police to restore order becomes difficult. In such an event, both the sides tend to be offenders, having committed some offence or the other (like wrongful confinement, voluntarily causing hurt on a person, act of intimidation, etc) under the criminal law. Parties in such a situation may be two 'powerful' individuals, or groups or even communities, in which case the police are almost invariably accused of partisanship. Therefore, in order to avoid a tricky situation as well as for rendering justice, the police take up 'cross-cases' against both the parties for the alleged offences committed by them during the skirmish. It often happens that both the parties are charge-sheeted in cross-cases for almost the same kind of offences in one particular incident.

12. What are the actions can a policeman or officer take against a suspected foreigner in his jurisdiction?

The world has become a global village due to a scientific and technological revolution in recent years. People are now tending to do globe trotting, although for different reasons. There are tourists visiting India purely for the purpose of seeing places. There are also people coming here for trade, commerce and industry. A good many come for educational purposes. These are all legitimate visits. But, at the same time, there are foreigners coming this country for espionage, drug-trafficking, gun running and similar ulterior purposes. Foreigners on visit to India are from all continents – Asia, Europe, Africa, Americas and Australia. There has been, in recent times, an increasing incidence of young people coming to India from African countries for drug trade. The police, therefore, need be very watchful about foreigners and be ready to take appropriate actions when called for.

While courtesy should be the hallmark of a policeman's conduct, especially when he is dealing with a foreigner, he should, at the same time, be firm. A policeman below the rank of Sub-Inspector may temporarily detain a foreigner suspected by him as having committed an offence, but he must immediately report to his superior about the matter. A Sub-Inspector or some officer above him should make an enquiry as to the papers – like the Passport, the Visa, the Restricted Area Permit (where applicable), etc - of the foreigner and satisfy himself they are in order. If not, a case will lie under Section 14 of the Foreigners Act 1946 and the foreigner may be arrested. It is the standard practice that arrest of a foreigner is reported up the ladder to the State Government for onward transmission to the Government of India.

Further, if the investigating police officer of a Foreigners Act case needs any information from a foreign government in regard to the case he has been handling, he has to send across the requisition through the proper channel, up to the MEA. No direct correspondence with a foreign government by an official is allowed.

13. How should the police handle a land dispute?

Land dispute is always a tricky subject for the police. Under ordinary circumstances, the police have nothing to do with it since it is a civil matter pertaining to land rights and occupation of land. These are subjects for revenue officials and civil courts. But in India, it always is an explosive matter, which leads very easily to a breach of the peace, involving criminal trespass, rioting, murder, etc. – all in a fit of rage or under cool calculations. Therefore, in all cases of land dispute, the police should take utmost care and take preventive action against any breach of the peace.

Sections 144 and 145 CrPC are the related procedural laws under which the police can initiate preventive measures through the Executive Magistrate concerned. Section 144 CrPC allows the clamping *suo motu* of prohibitory orders on a party in a land dispute. When the actual possession of a plot of land tends to be highly disputable, the police could submit a report to an Executive Magistrate to adjudicate on the actual possession of the land in question, pending any civil suit in respect of the title to the plot of land. (Section 145 CrPC).

14. Crimes against SC/ST are rampant in India despite the passing of more than 60 years of our Constitution. Is there any special law in the country to deal with the menace?

Crimes against the under-privileged classes or communities by so-called higher castes have been prevalent in India for centuries. It is a kind of violence-ridden apartheid that is in practice even now.

Such atrocities include dumping of excreta, carcasses or obnoxious substances in the victim's house or compound, stripping the victims (including women) naked or painting their faces with black tar, etc on flimsy excuses, forcibly grabbing their land, getting public servants to use their legal powers to harass them, putting them to bonded labour, falsely implicating them in criminal cases, intentionally humiliating, or assaulting them (even sexually in case of women), barring their access to or fouling sources of water and sundry other social crimes. Such hate crimes are more rampant in the plains areas rather than in the hills. The Untouchability Act 1955 was the first legislative measure to prevent such nauseating social crimes against the weaker sections of the society but it did not make much headway.

Alarmed at the growing incidence of notorious crimes against the SCs and the STs, Parliament passed the Scheduled Castes and the Scheduled Tribes (Prevention of Atrocities) Act 1989 to empower the state to take adequate measures to punish the guilty. It, *inter alia*, provided for stringent punishment for the persons committing such offences, to the extent of five years of imprisonment and fine for one single offence of this kind, and enhanced punishment for repetition of the same. The Act prohibits 'anticipatory bail' for the offenders and only Special Courts at the level of District and Sessions Judge could try them. The Act also provides for the requisite machinery and prescribed a mechanism to prevent the occurrence of such crimes. The State of UP has recorded a rather high number of cases under the law.

15. What is the concept of 'shoot at sight'? How is it dealt with in practice?

The idea is mooted during a situation when law and order is supposed to have broken down completely.

There is sometimes an outbreak of rioting or violent disturbance in certain urban or semi-urban areas, originating from a small or a big reason. Feeding on the grievances or fears of the people, or driven by baseless rumours or agent provocateurs, such riots often escalate to even rural areas, engulfing a larger population that may include several communities or groups. Such an outbreak results in loss of scores of lives and destruction of property and may even continue for days on end.

CrPC provides for powers to the Executive Magistracy to deal with such situations under Section 144, which essentially is prohibitory in character. When a prohibitory order under Section 144, - like one prohibiting an assembly, at a public place, of five or more persons with or without weapons, - does not have the desired effect, the order is made more stringent by imposition of 'Curfew". This is done under the same section of law.[2]

There are, however, situations when even an order of 'curfew' does not deter rioters from coming on to the streets to carry on with their mayhem. In such cases, the expression 'shoot at sight' is announced to scare away the rioters. But examined legally, such an order cannot be given effect to, because it would be negation of the affected person's Right to Life under Article 21 of the Constitution. In a hypothetical case, an innocent person may have come out on a curfew-bound road for some pressing reasons without being aware of the possible consequences and therefore the security forces or the police will have no right to shoot him 'at sight' right away.

16. What are the differences between Protected Area Permit (PAP)/Restricted Area Permit (RAP) and Inner Line Permit (ILP)?

The Foreigners (Protected Areas) Order 1958 requires that persons who are not Indian citizens will have to obtain PAP if they want to visit (1) certain parts of Jammu and Kashmir, (2) certain parts of Himachal Pradesh, (3) certain parts of Uttarakhand, and (4) any place in Arunachal Pradesh, Nagaland, Manipur and Mizoram.

Under the same Order, foreigners will require RAP to visit the Andaman & Nicobar Islands and parts of Sikkim. It was only sometime back the States of Assam, Meghalaya and Tripura have been removed from the list of places that required foreigners to obtain RAP before any visit.

The above system in force as a security measure in consideration of the sensitivity of the frontier areas involved. PAP and RAP are issued by the Ministry of Home Affairs.

ILP, on the other hand, is applicable only to Indian Citizens. It is a measure for the protection of the land, culture, and customary laws of the tribal people of the northeastern States of Arunachal Pradesh, Mizoram, Nagaland and Manipur. Imposed by the British government by the Bengal Eastern Frontier Regulation Act 1873,

---

2 The Executive Magistrate, at the same time, may proceed to disperse an unlawful assembly under Section 129 CrPC by use of force, which may include the use of tear gas, batons and even firing by the police.

the system was intended to keep the tribes concerned protected from cultural onslaught and economic exploitation by people living in more developed areas. ILP is issued by the state government concerned.

17. Do the police have any duty to an abandoned or neglected child?

An abandoned or neglected child needs care and protection. The Juvenile Justice (Care and Protection of Children) Act 2000 behoves the State government to set up a Child Welfare Committee (CWC) in every district in the State. The State government will also take all necessary measures to set up 'children's homes' in every district or group of districts for children in need of care and protection during the pendency of any inquiry and subsequently for their care, treatment, education training, development and rehabilitation.

Under Section 32 of the Act, the police, among many others, have been assigned the duty to produce before the CWC any child who is in need for care and protection. Obviously, the police will also have to extend all co-operation to the CWC in making the child secure and cared for. The time limit given for such production is 24 hours.

Appendix 1

Important Rules & Orders[1]

A. Assam Civil Services Conduct Rules 1965

1. These rules are applicable to all government servants appointed by the state government.
2. Every government servant shall at all times (a) maintain absolute integrity, (b) maintain devotion to duty, (c) do nothing which is unbecoming of a government servant.
3. The rules prohibit government servants:
   - (a) to accept gifts;
   - (b) to accept special public demonstration or presents in his honour;
   - (c) to criticise the government through the media or otherwise;
   - (d) to accept or organise public contribution of funds;
   - (e) to consume intoxicating drinks or drugs publicly or in contravention of law;
   - (f) to speculate in stocks, shares, investments etc;
   - (g) to engage in private trade or employment;
   - (h) to prosecute further studies without the permission of the government;
   - (i) to incur indebtedness or insolvency;
   - (j) to unauthorisedly communicate information to any person or body;

---

1 The Rules and Orders prevalent in Assam and quoted herein are more or less similar to those in other States and Union Territories.

(k) to maintain unauthorised connection with the press or the media;

(l) to appear unauthorisedly before any committee;

(m) to take part in politics or elections;

(n) to secure employment for his family members in a government undertaking by using official influence;

(o) to participate in demonstration or strike;

(p) to accept membership of an unrecognized association or any association the activities of which are prejudicial to the sovereignty and integrity of India or public order or morality;

(q) to contract a second marriage when the first marriage subsists.

3. Government may, however, make exceptions to the rules in an individual case on consideration of facts and circumstances of the particular case.

B. Assam Services (Confidential Rolls) Rules, 1990

1. These rules provide for writing of an annual confidential report on the government servants of and above a certain rank in different departments of the state government.

2. There are three authorities in connection with the writing, review and acceptance of the annual report called ACR.

3. The Confidential Roll comprises the following:

(a) the ACR for the year (calendar year or the financial year as the case may be),

(b letters of appreciation received by the government servant during the year,

(c) copy of the order imposing any penalty on the government servant after conclusion of a DP.

(d) copy of an order giving a 'warning' or conveying displeasure or reprimand to the government servant,

(e) record of approved course of study or training undertaken,

The ACR is written in a given *proforma.*

4. Recording, Review and Acceptance of ACR

(a) in the event of the retirement of the recording officer, the reviewing officer will record and review the ACR.

(b) in the event of the retirement of the reviewing officer, the accepting officer will review and accept the ACR.

(c) in the event of the retirement of the accepting officer, the remarks of the reviewing officer will be final.

(d) in the event of the retirement of both the reviewing and the accepting officers, the remarks of the recording officer shall be final.

(e) in the event of the retirement of both the recording and the reviewing officers, the accepting officer shall record, review and accept the ACR.

(f) in the event of the retirement of all the three concerned officers, a certificate to that effect will be kept in the Roll.

5. Where there is an adverse remark in the Roll, the reviewing officer will communicate the same to the government servant concerned within one month of its acceptance by the accepting authority.

6. The government servant can represent against the adverse remark to the state government or to the authority next above the accepting authority within sixty days of the date of receipt of the ACR by him. The final order given by the said authority or the government will be placed in the Roll.

It is to be mentioned here that non-communication of adverse remarks given in the ACR is a violation of the rules of natural justice and therefore justiciable.

C. Use of Red Light and Siren

In writ petition (PI.L) No.3807/1999, the hon'ble Gauhati High Court passed an order (dated 9. 2. 2000) that unauthorized use of red light and siren should be checked and stopped without delay. The hon'ble court further directed that the traffic regulations, wherever any risk factor is involved, be such that avoidable inconvenience to the public should be avoided and it should be implemented in such a manner that even the flow of traffic should not be affected more than necessary and there may not be any mishandling of the members of the public nor they be treated disgracefully.

The following dignitaries/categories of persons are entitled to use red lights on the front top of their vehicles:

1. President,
2. Vice-President,
3. Governor/Lt-Governor,
4. Heads of Indian Missions abroad,
5. Prime Minister, other Cabinet Ministers, Ministers of State and Deputy Ministers of the Union; Chief Ministers, Cabinet Ministers, MoSs and Deputy Ministers of States,
6. Speaker /Deputy Speaker of Lok Sabha /Legislative Assemblies,
7. Deputy Chairperson of Rajya Sabha,
8. Chief Justice /Judges of the Supreme Court/High Courts,
9. State Chief Secretary,
10. Director General of Police,
11. Pilot cars,
12. Fire Brigade vehicles,
13. Ambulance,
14. Lok Ayukta,
15. Chairperson and Vice Chairperson of Central Administrative Tribunal,

By Notification No TMV.438/87/164 dated 12 .07. 2002, the Government of Assam has included the following dignitaries also in the above category:

1. Leader of Opposition in the State Assembly,
2. Lok Ayukta
3. CEMs of Autonomous Councils,
4. Additional Chief Secretary.

D. Prosecution of Members of the Police and Other Forces: Protection U/S 197 (2) CrPC

By a State amendment of section 197(2) CrPC under sub-section (3) of the same section, the Government of Assam acquired the power (with effect from 5.6.1980) to direct that the members of the police and para-military forces engaged in maintenance of public order in the state would get protection from frivolous prosecution for acts done in course of duty ((Act 3 of 1980).

In exercise of the power as aforesaid, the Government of Assam issued a Notification that (1) all ranks of Assam Police, (2) all ranks of Home Guards, (3) all para-military forces on law and order duties in Assam will be protected under section 197(2) CrPC and cannot be prosecuted in the court of law without the sanction of the state government.

[Vide Notification No. HMA.280 /88/70 dated 18. 12. 1995]

The Supreme Court in WP (criminal) No. 340—343 of 1993 (Vineet Narain and Others *vs* Union of India and Another) has given the following direction vide its judgement dated 18.12.1997:

'Time limit of three months in grant of sanction for prosecution must be strictly adhered to. However, additional time of one month may be allowed where consultation is required with the Attorney General or any other law officer in the AG's office.'

The Government of India has since brought to the attention of all state governments and union territory administrations the above direction of the Supreme Court for implementation.

E. Norms of Journalistic Conduct

The Constitution of India has given to the citizens of the country the fundamental right to freedom of speech and expression under Article 19(1)(a) and, at the same time, makes its use subject to reasonable restrictions. The state can therefore make laws imposing certain restrictions on the media in the interest of sovereignty, integrity and security of the state, friendly relations with foreign countries, public order, decency and morality.

As a follow-up to the above, the Press Council of India was established in 1979 with the object of preserving the freedom of the press and improving the standard of newspapers and other print media. The said Council has accordingly developed and brought in place a code of conduct for all newspaper houses and journalists during the last two and a half decades. Since the time it was established, the Council has been imposing on the newspaper industry and journalists a series of self-regulatory principles.

The following are a summary of the principal guidelines given by the Council:

1. The press shall refuse to publish inaccurate, baseless and distorted materials.

2. Verification should be done of reports received, especially in respect of individual citizens.
3. Defamatory news should not be published, especially against individuals. Truth is no defence.
4. The press should not publish any thing derogatory against a dead person.
5. Due restraint and caution to be maintained in forming a opinion and coming to a conclusion.
6. Nothing should be done to influence the conduct of investigation or prosecution by public officials.
7. Investigating agencies must not leak out or disclose information or disinformation on the conduct of investigation.
8. The Official Secrets Act 1923 binds the press and the media also.
9. The press should not intrude upon the privacy of individuals.
10. Things relating to a person's home, family, religion, health, sexuality, personal life, and private affairs are covered by the concept of privacy.
11. While reporting crimes (involving rape, abduction or kidnap of women, sexual assault on children and so on), the names/ photographs of victims shall not be published. There is a caution against identification.
12. Children, who were born due to sexual abuse, forcible marriage or illicit-sexual union, are not to be identified or photographed.
13. The press shall not tape-record anyone's conversation without his consent.
14. Newspapers should not present their conjectures as a statement of fact.
15. Newspapers should not pass a judgement on guilt or innocence of a person.
16. A newspaper should not identify itself with a party in a controversy.
17. When a factual error is detected, the newspaper should publish the correction promptly. Similarly, it should publish any contradiction given by an aggrieved party.
18. Newspapers are not to publish any vulgar thing, including vulgar advertisements.

19. Violence is not to be glorified.
20. Social evils are not to be glorified.
21. Communal clashes should be reported with due caution and restraint and in a manner conducive to peace and amity. Headings should not be provocative.
22. References to caste and community should be avoided in reporting.
23. Religious figures not to be portrayed in adverse light.
24. Incorrect maps must not be published as it may affect the territorial integrity of the country.
25. The interest of the nation is to be kept paramount in all reporting.
26. The press should not criticise judicial acts of courts of law.

WE have to remember one adage " Eternal vigilance is the price of liberty" The press is the standard bearer of freedom and it should do nothing to abuse its own freedom.

FSC/ST Reservation

The Assam Scheduled Caste and Scheduled Tribes (Reservation of Vacancies in Services and Posts) Act 1978 came into force with effect from 1st July 1979.

Secondly, the Governor of Assam issued an order (under Notification No. TAD/OBC/141/91/60, Dated 30th June 1993) effecting reservation of 15 per cent of the vacancies in all posts under the State and in services connected with the affairs of the State and its Public Sector Undertakings for members of the Other Backward Classes (OBCs including MOBCs - More Other Backward Classes).

As per the schedule of the said Act and the Order, a 20-point Roster is to be prepared and maintained at all offices of the state government.

- In the said Roster,
- the first and the eleventh vacancies are reserved for the scheduled tribes (plains),
- the third and the twelfth vacancies are reserved for the scheduled castes,
- the seventh vacancy is reserved for the scheduled tribes (hills), and

- the second, eighth and fifteenth vacancies are reserved for the OBCs/MOBCs.

The proviso to section 5 of the ASCST (RVSP) Act 1978 and the Order on reservation of OBCs/MOBCs mentioned above have given power to the government to implement the reservation policy. As such, the 20-point Roster is to be prepared and maintained compulsorily by the authority concerned at all state government offices to do justice to SCs, STs and OBCs in the matter of employment.

G. Treatment of Non-criminal Lunatics (NCL)

In Writ Petition (Cr) No. 237/1989 (Sheila Barse vs Union of India and Others), the Supreme Court in its order dated 17.8.1993 declared that the detention of NCLs in police custody or jail custody was illegal and unconstitutional. The apex court further directed that the judicial magistrate before whom the NCL is produced will have him/her examined by a professional in mental health/psychiatrist and send him or her to the nearest hospital for care.

As a follow-up to the above, the Government of Assam vide its Notification No. HMA.243/93/pt/5 dated 16.5.1994 has ordered that no NCL shall be detained in any prison on any ground whatsoever under the provisions of Indian Lunacy Act 1912.

H. Mission Statement of Assam Police

"Our objective is to

Maintain order, prevent and detect crime by enforcing law firmly and impartially without fear or favour, prejudice or vindictiveness.

Maintain integrity and discipline of the highest order in sincere performance of duties in accordance with the law and the Constitution and respect the rights of citizens as guaranteed by it.

Strive to build up a strong police-public bond in order to encourage community participation in law enforcement and promote harmony and a spirit of brotherhood amongst all segments of society, transcending religious, linguistic, social and regional diversities and to remove practices derogatory to the dignity of women and disadvantaged sections of society.

Strive to be courteous and well-mannered at all times, develop self-restraint and be truthful and honest in thought and deed, in both personal and official life.

I. 'Pollution Under Control' Certificate

By Notification No. TMV.45/96/204 dated 23.6. 2000, the Government of Assam have ordered as follows:

After expiry of a period of one year from the date on which a motor vehicle was first registered, it shall carry a valid 'pollution under control certificate' issued by a privatised pollution check station authorised for the purpose by the government.

Failure on the above will attract penalty under section 190 of MV Act 1988 as amended.

J. Despatch of Materials to Forensic Lab

The Gauhati High Court has held that the practice of investigating officers of the police sending through the court the materials and articles seized during investigation to the Forensic Science Laboratory for examination was objectionable. It said it was no part of the duty of the judicial magistrates to step in at the stage of investigation.

The investigating agency has therefore the full responsibility to take care of the incriminating materials and have them examined at the FSL to come to a conclusion on the facts of the case concerned.

[Criminal Appeal No. 55 of 1995 and No.68 of 1995]

K. Special Police Officers Under IT (P) Act

The Government of Assam vide its Notification No. HMA.437/94/35 dated 29. 10. 1994 have declared all Deputy Superintendents of Police (Headquarters) and Sub-divisional Police Officers in Assam as 'Special Police Officers' (SPOs) under section 13 (I) of Immoral Traffic (P) Act 1956 as amended.

In addition, all Inspectors of Police, who are in charge of police stations and all Inspector level officers of the CID were also declared SPOs under the Act.

L. Handcuffing Of Prisoners

In WP (civil) No. 22/1995 (the Citizens for Democracy *vs* State of Assam and others), the Supreme Court ordered as follows:

1. Handcuffs and fetters shall not be forced on a prisoner - convicted or under-trial - while lodged in a jail or while being transported or in transit from one jail to another or from jail to court or back from

court to jail. The police or jail authorities on their own shall have no authority to direct the handcuffing of an inmate of a jail or during transport from one jail to another or from jail to court and back.

2. Where the police or jail authorities have a well-grounded basis for drawing a strong inference that a particular prisoner is likely to break out of custody, the said prisoner will have to be produced before the magistrate concerned and a prayer for permission to handcuff the prisoner shall be made. -- The magistrate may grant permission to handcuff the prisoner.
3. In all cases where a person arrested is produced before a magistrate and remand is given by the magistrate, the person concerned shall not be handcuffed unless a special order is obtained from the magistrate.
4. A person arrested on a warrant of arrest shall not be handcuffed unless the police had obtained orders of the magistrate to that effect.
5. If the police officer making an arrest without warrant is satisfied that it was necessary to handcuff the arrested person, he may do so till he is taken to the police station or produced before the court. Further use of handcuff can only be under orders of the magistrate.
6. Any violation of the above orders will be a contempt of court and will also be punishable under the law.

Issue of NBW During Investigation and Remand to Police Custody After Filing of Charge-Sheet

In Criminal Appeal No. 157 –159- 97, the Supreme Court has ruled as follows vide order dated 7.5.1997:

1. Non-bailable warrant of arrest (NBW) can be issued by the court even during investigation against a person who has been evading arrest. It need not wait till the filing of charge-sheet.
2. Police remand can be given by the court in respect of an accused who is arrested subsequent to filing of charge-sheet.

N. Disposal of Dead Bodies by the Police

The Government of Assam have amended the Assam Police Manual, Part V, and incorporated Rule 168 (c) in it laying down guidelines for disposal of dead bodies by the police in connection with police cases, vide Notification No HMA.430/26/97 dated 2.1.1998. The points made in the guidelines are follows:

1. Identified bodies are to be made over to the relatives of the deceased unless the District Magistrate or a Magistrate concerned orders otherwise in the interest of public order. Close relatives may be allowed to be present if the police are to do the final disposal, which should be done with due reverence and decency.
2. In case of an identified body, the close relatives are to be ordinarily given 48 hours to receive it. If no claimant appears, the police will dispose it of as per the above procedure.
3. In case of an unidentified body, the police will give wide publicity giving relatives 72 hours to claim the body. If no one turns up within this time, the police will dispose of the body obtaining an order to that effect from the DM or the SDM. If there is doubt about the religious denomination of the deceased, he will be buried so that exhumation may be done later if required.
4. In all cases of disposal of a body by the police, a Magistrate has to remain present.
5. In case of custodial death, the relatives may be given 72 hours to come and receive the body.
6. In the intimation sent by the police to the relatives of a deceased person, the time and place of death and the circumstances leading to the death of the deceased should be clearly mentioned.
7. The expenditures incurred in transportation, preservation, making of coffin and final disposal of the body will be borne by the police officially.

Appendix 2

Miscellany

There is a saying that ordinary people learn things and gain experience about life through a trial and error process. However, it also says that wise people learn lessons from others' experiences and put them to their own use. Some of the points noted in Appendix II are the experiences gained and experimentations done by others elsewhere.

1. Delhi Police to take NGO's help in tackling rape cases

In a radical departure from the existing practices, the Delhi Police have asked NGOs (Non-Governmental Organisations) to help them in the investigation of rape cases, especially those involving minors, right from the time they are reported.

Rape is the most complex and sensitive of crimes as it brings with it immense social and psychological damage to the victim. This damage often becomes a barrier in the process of criminal justice.

Besides the Investigating Officer (I/O), the rape victim will be visited by a team comprising a counsellor, a social worker and a doctor. While the I/O will take charge of the crime aspect, others will begin what is called *social investigation.*

Each case will be under the supervision of a gazetted officer. The 'crime against women' cell at the district headquarters will be functioning as a crisis management center. The police will visit the victim in civilian clothes. The counsellors will prepare an assessment report in each case and indicate the extent of trauma of the victim and the level of intervention needed, including financial and other aids for rehabilitation.

The team mentioned above will remain associated with the victim during investigation and right up to the end of the court proceedings.

Collection of evidence in rape cases is tricky. The police station shall have the special kits required for the purpose.

Doctors will be asked to take three 'vaginal swabs' as samples for conducting DNA test, if needed.

This approach will help build confidence in the minds of the victim and her family members and will help the police to secure conviction.

Being usually in trauma after an incident of rape, the victim normally does not open up to co-operate with the police in investigation. A rape victim tends to blame herself and the parents also tend to blame the victim for the happening. This makes the situation very complex. Here comes the role of counsellors.

[*The Times of India*, 01.06.2000]

2. Prison condition

Former Chairperson of the National Human Rights Commission Justice MN Venkatachaliah has described the conditions in Indian prisons as 'dismal'. They are like penal dustbins.

A person in custody in any civilised society cannot be reduced to the status of a non-person. The prison or 'lock-up' conditions should be compatible with human dignity and conducive to social mainstreaming.

[*The Times of India*, 05.05.2000]

In a warning to prison authorities, the Supreme Court has ruled that death of a detained person due to unhygienic conditions in jail would make officials liable to prosecution for custodial death. This is a significant departure from the earlier position in the matter as such charges used to be brought only when death was caused by torture or physical assault. The ruling came on a petition filed by Indu Jain and the MP Government, both challenging a High Court verdict acquitting officials of custody death charges.

The brief of the case was that officials attached to Lok Ayukta had arrested one RK Jain on bribery charges and put him, a known asthma patient, in an unused room that had no ventilation. Jain had a severe asthma attack due to the dust in the cobwebbed room. He was rushed to a hospital only on the next day in a state of coma. The same day, Jain expired. Hearing the case, a bench of the apex court, comprising Justices Altamas Kabir and Markandey Katju, ordered that the officials concerned would be tried for causing death of the victim by negligence. It also ordered that a *prima facie* charge of inflicting injury on the detained person would fastened on the erring officials as it was clear that he died of asphyxia on account of detention in unhygienic conditions despite his respiratory problems.

[*The Times of India*, 07.12.2008]

3. Rape or cheating?

In a recent case, a starlet accused a film director of rape and criminal intimidation. The case has thrown up the following important issues:

Can sexual intercourse, which is consented to on a promise of marriage, be treated as rape?

No, say lawyers.

They say that such a case may at best attract the offence of cheating under Section 415 of IPC.

Even here the question of motive or intention comes. If at the time of making such a promise, the offender did not intend to get married, it would amount to cheating.

Cheating originates from misrepresentation of facts. In a typical case of cheating, a sex worker assured a client that she did not have venereal disease and sleeping with him, infected him. She was found guilty of cheating.

Rulings by the Supreme Court say that a mere failure to keep a promise cannot be taken as cheating unless such intention was shown when the inducement was given.

If a married man promises marriage to a girl concealing his marital status, it amounts to cheating.

A remedy for a broken promise could be a suit for damages under the civil law of torts.

It should also be clear that if a woman submits to sexual intercourse with an aim to benefiting from it, she herself is guilty of moral turpitude.

[*The Times of India*, 04.08.2004]

4. Security for witness

Witnesses generally lack faith in the justice delivery system for their own safety and security. Attacks on victims and witnesses are a common feature in criminal litigation in India.

In the backdrop of this problem, the Delhi High Court has issued guidelines for safety of witnesses who receive threats in all cases punishable with death or life imprisonment.

(i) Witness has to move an application before the Member-Secretary of Delhi Legal Services Authority (DLSA).

(ii) The Member-Secretary of the DLSA will decide the extent and duration of protection.

(iii) The nature of risk to the witness would be considered.

(iv) The importance of the witness and the value of his testimony would be taken into account.

(v) Every witness will be made aware of these guidelines by the investigating officer concerned.

In a case study it was found that a witness had sought protection but was denied the same. Later he changed the statement to the detriment of the case. Moreover, the court charged him for giving false evidence in the case in which he was a prosecution witness.

[*The Times of India*, 22.02.2005]

5. Trafficking in women

The following are the findings of Ms Pamela Shifman, an associate director of an international human rights organisation 'Equality Now', while on visit to India:

(i) About 50,000 women and children are trafficked to the US every year. The majority is from South Asia and South East Asia.

(ii) Under the laws it is mostly the victims who are punished, not the perpetrators. Under the Indian law, women are four times more likely to be arrested than men are.

(iii) Women are vulnerable to poverty and discrimination.

(iv) The customers who create the demand should be punished. In Sweden, it is the sex users and not the sex workers who are punished. It is illegal to purchase sex there. It is not illegal to be in prostitution.

(v) The media should warn women of the possibility of trafficking.

(vi) Domestic violence and trafficking are interlinked. When women are victims of violence, they become vulnerable to trafficking because they want to flee their homes. Similarly, children, who are sexually abused in their homes, are more vulnerable to traffickers.

(vii) The police normally try to avoid intervening in domestic violence on the ground that it is a family matter. Similarly, they say prostitution is the oldest profession and so, why intervene?

(viii) Domestic violence exists in every class, educated or uneducated. Men choose to batter women. Their attitude needs to be changed.

(ix) Laws should be enforced. This will send a message to the wrong doer that wrongs will not be tolerated.

(x) Trafficking in the guise of marriage is also a big industry.

(xi) Government officials and NGOs should co-operate with one another.

[*The Times of India*, 03.01.2002]

6. New technique to track down rapists

According to the research findings at the National University, La Jolla, California, a new forensic technique has been developed, by which rapists, who use condoms to protect themselves from being identified, can now be tracked down. The time of death of the sperms in condoms discarded and recovered at or near the crime spot can help the police pinpoint the time of rape. This can be used to corroborate the victim's testimony.

[*The Telegraph*, 21.03.2005]

7. Rape evidence glare on Doctor

The chief medical officer of a civil hospital at Ahmedabad was arrested by the police and remanded in judicial custody after alleged destruction of evidence under Section 201 of the IPC in connection with a case of gang rape. The doctor was arrested after a 600-page charge-sheet was filed by the police against 12 people. Officials said that the doctor had deliberately failed to collect the 'vaginal swab' of the victim, which could have been a crucial piece of evidence in the case. Collection of the same is mandatory under the regulations in such cases.

[*The Telegraph*, 29.03.2004]

8. Action against Police officer and Medical officer

On the intervening night of July 12 and 13, 1990, at about 2 am, some miscreants entered the St Mary's Convent School at Gajranla in UP, committed rape on two sisters of the convent and assaulted the other inmates. They also looted Rs 1,11,000/-, which was kept in the house for payment of salaries of the staff. The case was perfunctorily investigated by the police and charge-sheeted against four accused persons.

However, the incident was brought to the notice of the Supreme Court by a PIL. The Supreme Court then ordered a CBI investigation, which found that the case was not investigated properly. It also pointed out specific lapses on the part of the investigating police officers and the lady medical officer concerned. They were held responsible for destruction of vital evidence in the case. Thereupon the Supreme Court ordered the UP Government to suspend the above officers and initiate disciplinary action with a view to imposing major penalties on them. It also awarded compensation of Rs 2,50,000/- each to the victims of rape and Rs 1,00,000/- each to the other victims and directed the State Government to recover the total amount of money from the guilty officers.

[Gudalure MJ Cherian *vs* Union of India 1995 SCC (Cr) 925]

9. Assault of *detenu* in Court compound – Contempt of Court

On January 24, 1994, a CBI *detenu*, Satish Das, who was to be produced before the Supreme Court on its order, was beaten up and kicked by CBI constables right in the precincts of the Court. Two Inspectors, who were on supervisory duty, kept mum. When the matter was brought to the notice of the Court, it ordered medical examination of the *detenu*. The latter was found very weak physically. The SP, CBI, tendered an apology as he had failed to control the misconduct of his subordinates.

The apex court invoked contempt jurisdiction to punish the police officers and observed that the incident was symptomatic of the degeneration of the police in the respect for law, human dignity and human rights. The Court issued a reprimand to the SP, fined the Inspectors Rs 1,000/- each and sentenced the constables to one month's imprisonment and fine of Rs 1,000/- each.

[Jaspal Singh *vs* State of UP 1995 SCC (Cr) 832]

10. UP's dowry district turns a corner – courtesy an innovative police programme

Etah is Uttar Pradesh's dowry district. With dowry death and harassment cases going up each year, the police realised that something innovative had to be done. The result was operation *Didi*.

In the first ten months of the year 2004 (till October), there were 98 cases of dowry harassment and 46 dowry deaths. Prior to that, in 2002 alone, there were 78 recorded dowry deaths.

Against the backdrop of these happenings, the police started and held counselling sessions every Sunday in the affected areas. The outcome was overwhelming. "There has not been a single case of dowry death since October 2004 and our Sundays till June next year are booked with 560 matters listed for hearing," said SSP, Etah.

The police are not alone. About 30 people, including 14 women, were designated as 'Special Police Officers' for the job. They are workers, doctors, teachers and so on. It has been seen by the counselors that about 40 per cent of the complaints were not dowry-related at all but owed to lack of trust between the parties. What is therefore required is concerted counselling to get the warring parties into an emotional reunion.

[*The Indian Express*, 26.12.2004]

11. Arrests by armed forces and making over the arrested person to the police

NHRC Case No. 2563/94-95 emanated from the custodial death of one Kheshiho Sumi, an NSCN (I-M) activist in Nagaland. The brief of the story is that on November 12, 1994, Sumi was arrested 'on suspicion' by the Assam Rifles at Purana Bazaar and on November 14, while he was being taken for an 'operation', he allegedly jumped out of the running vehicle in a bid to escape. Injured Sumi was taken to the Dimapur Civil Hospital where he was declared dead.

The NHRC reviewed the case and concluded that the armed force were responsible for the custodial death and asked the unit concerned to pay a compensation of Rupees One Lakh to Sumi's dependents.

The Commission observed that the detention of the deceased was illegal. He should have been handed over to the police immediately after arrest.

Secondly, taking him out for operational purpose was a part of an attempt to investigate the alleged offence of the arrested person, a matter beyond the jurisdiction of the armed forces.

12. Goof up in investigation

[A] A Chinese man badly beaten and jailed for his wife's 'murder' has been freed after she turned up not only alive but with another husband, the domestic media in China said. The lady had disappeared after a domestic quarrel and when a woman's body was found in a local reservoir, the husband was detained on suspicion of killing his wife. The body was so decomposed that it could not be properly identified but a local court found him 'guilty of murder' and sentenced him to death. A provincial court later commuted the sentence to 15 years in prison. The accused husband in the case was coerced into confessing to 'the lady's murder' and badly beaten in prison.

[*The Times of India*, 05. 04. 2005]

* *The lesson to be drawn from this case is very clear. Suspicion cannot take the place of proof. An error in the investigation of a murder case may even take an innocent life.*

[B] A villager named Hari Muduli in Orissa spent nearly five and a half years in jail impersonating as his younger brother Kuma, an accused in a 1999 murder case. When the matter came to light and the imprisoned person's identity was established, he was released. Hari did all this for his brotherly love. The police have now been able to nab the culprit after a long search. He has now confessed to the crime. Explaining the goof up, the SP Koraput has said, 'Hari had identified himself as Kuma; all along he stuck to his false identity. But when Kuma got nabbed in a petty offence, the skeleton tumbled out.'

[*The Times of India*, 20. 04. 2005]

* *This is an example of a serious goof up by the police in a murder case in India, like the one in China recorded in the previous entry.*

13. Trafficking in women and children

It is difficult to figure out the number of women and children who have been trafficked into India over the years from the neighbouring countries. People are trafficked also across the state borders within the country. NGOs estimate that at least 7000 girls are trafficked into India from Nepal every year. They end up in brothels of Metros and other towns and are condemned to a life of deprivation and torture. A similar flow of innocent children and girls has been taking place from Bangladesh also. All this is Rape for Profit.

[*The Times of India*, 25. 03. 2005.]

14. Railways ordered to pay widow

After 22 years of the death of a Railway gangman, his widow realised that she was entitled to a family pension.

The Railways had refused her plea on many grounds, including the time lapse between the death and the claim. Andhra Pradesh High Court allowed her plea partly, saying that she would get the pension only from 1992 when she filed the case. The Supreme Court now held that she was entitled to the family pension right from November 21, 1969 (the day the gangman had died) and directed the Railways to pay up all arrears within three months. It also asked the Railways to pay a litigation cost of Rupees ten thousand to her.

Most significantly, the bench consisting of Justices NS Hegde and BP Singh ruled as follows:

" On the death of the husband of Mastan Bee, it was obligatory for her husband's employer, the Railways, to have computed the family pension payable to her and offer the same to her without her having to make a claim or without driving her to litigation. The very denial of the family pension to her by the Railways amounted to a violation of the fundamental right under Article 21 of the Constitution."

[*PTI*, 06. 12. 2002]

15. Court offers little to rape victims

It has been seen that in innumerable cases, the rape victim gets condemned to live a life of indignity, frustration and shame while the accused walks away with his head high being let off by the court. If past judgements are anything to go by, the Indian judicial system needs to do a lot of introspection. Here are a few cases the outcome of which has been very discouraging for anyone who cares for the victims of sexual assault:

Mathura, a 16-year-old tribal girl, was raped by two policemen in Chandrapur district of Maharashtra in the 1970s.These policemen had called Mathura to the police station, frightened the girl to give consent and raped her. The Sessions court decided the case in favour of the accused saying Mathura was a liar and that she was habituated to sexual intercourse. The Nagpur Bench of the Bombay High Court set aside the judgement and sentenced the policemen to five years and one year of imprisonment respectively. It said that passive submission due to fear induced by serious threats could not be construed as willingness in sexual intercourse. But the Supreme Court acquitted the policemen on the ground that Mathura had not raised an alarm at the time of the incident and there were no visible marks of injury on her body.

In another case, Sakina, a 16-year-old girl from Kerala, was lured away to Ernakulam with the promise of a job and forced into prostitution. She was kept in confinement for a good 18 months and was regularly raped by clients. She managed to file a petition before the High Court but it was quashed with the observation that it was improbable to believe that a man who desired to have sex on payment would come to a reluctant woman. The HC also cast aspersion on her character saying that 'the version of a woman of this character is not so sacrosanct as to be taken for granted.'

In the Bhanwari Devi case, a sessions judge remarked that the victim could not have been raped since she was a Dalit while the accused was from an upper caste.

In Md Habib *vs* the State, a High Court acquitted the accused on the ground that there was no injury on his private parts presuming thereby that the victim had not resisted.

However, the following judgments of the Supreme Court stand out as landmark guidelines in the rape law:

Haniffa Khatoon, a Bangladeshi national, was raped by some railway employees in Howrah in 1998. The SC asked the railways to pay her compensation and declared rape to be violation of fundamental right to live with dignity guaranteed under the Constitution.

The SC in another judgment has ruled that a rape accused could be convicted on the basis of the sole testimony of the victim.

[*The Times of India*, 25. 10. 2003]

* *Rape is a crime that negates the right of a woman to equality and dignity. Nothing can be more humiliating than this for a woman. The problem is entirely one sided. The rapist does not have to feel*

ashamed. Against this backdrop there are two important viewpoints for us to ponder upon:

A. *The accused should be deemed guilty unless he is able to prove his innocence.*

B. *The danger of rape will continue unless the rapists are punished publicly.*

16. Delay in lodging FIR in rape case

The courts cannot overlook the fact that in sexual offences, delay in lodging the FIR can be due to a variety of reasons, particularly the reluctance of the prosecutrix or her family members to go to the police and complain about the incident, which concerns the reputation and honour of the family. It is only after giving it a cool thought that a complaint of sexual offence is generally lodged.

[The Supreme Court in State of Punjab *vs* Gurmit Singh]

17. HC orders video-conferencing for rape victims

The Delhi High Court has directed that a rape victim should from now on be examined thorough video-conferencing or through CC TV to prevent the harassment and humiliation of the victim. Justice RC Chopra issued the directive to the lower judiciary and said that the courts should firmly step in to ensure that victims of sexual offence do not undergo a harrowing experience when cross-examined. 'The spate of questions put to them during cross-examination sometimes cross the limits of decency. These queries make them re-live the incident', the Judge observed. 'It happens in spite of holding the trial in camera because the presence of the prosecutor, the defence advocate and the accused is unavoidable', Justice Chopra said.

[*NE Reporter*, 01. 09. 2004]

18. A helping hand for Arunachal women and children

People from various walks of life have joined hands to launch Helping Hand, a voluntary organisation, in Arunachal Pradesh. They included social activists, advocates, educationists, doctors, journalists and policemen. This is to provide emotional support to women and children through counselling and career guidance to school dropouts and the like. Papum Pare district superintendent of police Robin Hibu, who conceived the idea, has said that the center has been set up to tackle the growing atrocities against women and children as well as the increasing number of cases of juvenile delinquency.

The center will adopt, among other things, the following agenda, *viz* (i) safe street campaign, (ii) free career guidance, (iii) coaching for bright students, (iv) imparting driving lessons (v) coaching for self-employment, etc. Action on domestic violence will also be a top priority item for the NGO.

[*The Times of India*, 24.04.2005]

19. 'Victim' of Rape and Murder returns with husband in tow

On police records teenager Sikha of West Tripura was raped and murdered but in reality she is not only alive but living a happy domestic life with her husband in Bangladesh. On June 1, 2005, the father of the girl Harendra Sarkar filed an FIR at the local Police Station that his 19-year-old daughter Sikha had been gang-raped and killed. He named four accused persons whom the police promptly picked up. They were later remanded to judicial custody. The arrested persons denied involvement but to no avail.

On June 27, to everybody's surprise, Sikha and her uncle (husband of her father's sister) Ratan Sarkar appeared at the police station and stated that they had got married and shifted to Bangladesh. This followed an affair between her uncle and herself and was done at the instance of her father when her pregnancy resulting from the affair came to be known. It has now been found that Haren Sarkar had filed the false case against the four innocent persons only to take advantage of the situation to settle old scores against the latter on account of a long-standing family feud.

[*The Times of India*, 02.07.2005]

**An important point that emerges from this incident is that the police should not simply rush to arrest persons accused in a crime without proper investigation. In the present case, the police action has been extremely callous and had a dangerous potential.*

20. Rape trial ends in lack of evidence

A city court has acquitted 3 persons accused of abduction and gang rape of a woman in a moving car in 1994 in Delhi. The trial court indicted the police of holding back crucial witnesses and found the alleged victim 'an unreliable witness'.

The accused trio had allegedly abducted the woman on the night of November 11, 1994 and raped her in a car. The court said; 'the woman kept changing her statement about the date of the incident, lodging of the complaint, details of the arrest, etc and glaring discrepancies had emerged making her story doubtful and unworthy of credence'. The prosecution did not examine the juice shop owner who, the woman claimed, was a witness to her abduction, nor her four friends to whom she had first narrated the incident.

The court further said, 'It is well-settled law that holding back available witnesses leads the court to draw adverse inference against the prosecution that if examined they would have deposed against the prosecution'.

[*The Times of India*, 25. 05. 2005]

**This is a typical instance of bungled investigation of a very serious criminal case. It should have been possible for both the investigating police and the public prosecutor concerned to maintain perfect co-ordination and to check and re-check the statements of the witnesses so that such glaring contradictions did not appear during the trial. There is also nothing to explain why the most vital witnesses in the case were not produced for examination during the trial.*

HC relief for man who spent five extra years in jail

***Jabalpur*:** Pooran Singh, a drug peddler, was arrested in the year 2000 under NDPS Act 1985 for alleged possession of *marijuana (ganja)* and was sentenced to 10 years in jail and a fine of Rs 1 lakh by the trial court concerned. On his appeal, the High Court reduced the prison term to three years and the fine to Rs 1,000. Since, by that time, the accused had already spent three years in prison, the High Court ordered his immediate release from jail. But the prison authorities failed to take notice of the order. It was only when one of his relatives moved an application in October 2008 that the prison authorities realised that Pooran Singh had been forced to serve five extra years in prison.

The victim, on release from jail, sent a letter to Justice AK Patnaik, Chief Justice of the High Court, narrating his ordeal. The letter was treated by the court as a PIL and it directed the state government to pay the victim a compensation of Rs three lakh within a period of three months. The court also allowed the petitioner to file separate civil suits for compensation for other losses and damages he suffered due to the callous attitude of the jail authorities.

[*The Times of India*, 18.03.2009]

* *It was a gross violation of the victim's fundamental right under Articles 21, 19 and 14 of the Constitution. Apart from paying compensation to him, the government on its own should hold an immediate enquiry into the incident, fix responsibility for the serious negligence on the part of the jail officials concerned and award exemplary punishment to them.*

Appendix 3

Some Administrative Points

- Senior officers have to assume a leading role through both personal example and superintendence over the functioning of the organisation.
- Public servants have to function within the ambit of law and within constitutional limits.
- Illegal orders are not binding on anybody.
- Oral orders should be confirmed in writing at the earliest opportunity.
- Officers should not be prisoners of routine but should rise above with imagination and initiative.
- Exemplary and deterrent action taken in a few bad cases tones up the administration and removes the necessity of large-scale penal action.
- A good administrator always does advance planning and sets goals for the rank and file.
- Once the goals are set, the next step is to fix a time-bound programme, implementation of which has to be monitored and reviewed from time to time.
- There should be greater reliance on discussion on personal level, rather than making needless correspondence and file references in the implementation of programmes.
- The head of the organisation has to be mindful of the need for prompt action in service matters, like disposal of appeals, regularisation of appointments, disposal of disciplinary cases, confirmation of service, fixing of seniority, pension,

etc. These measures are of top priority in human resource management and help raise the morale of the employees.

- Regular inspections and surprise checks help maintain the standard of functioning of the department or organisation concerned.
- Maximum possible delegation of powers to officers in the hierarchy builds up a sense of responsibility at all levels and things get going much faster.

Tips For Officers

- Do not apologise for making a reasonable demand.
- Do not over-qualify your statement.
- Do not shift responsibility of your statement to others.
- Be direct but polite.
- Think things through and conceptualise issues before stating them.
- Confront problems immediately.
- Choose your issues carefully.
- Separate anger from assertiveness.
- Use your home ground as far as possible.
- Use non-verbal cues. Maintain eye contact. And instead of re-stating your case, use silence for reinforcement.
- Avoid empty threats.
- Share your knowledge with others.
- Improve communication skill.
- Expel procrastination and take care of the concept of time management.
- Develop inter-personal skill.

Appendix 4

The Criminal Law (Amendment) Act 2013

The horrendous assault and gang-rape of a 23-year old girl – a medical student - in Delhi on December 16, 2012, followed by her horrific suffering and death in a Singapore hospital a few days later, shook the nation and its conscience. There followed throughout the months of December 2012 and January 2013 a tremendous upsurge of the people and a strident demand for a radical change in the country's rape law. The issue turned out to be not only one of strengthening the law relating to rape but also about comprehensive action by the state against all forms of gender violence, including various forms of attack on the modesty of women, stripping, voyeurism, harassment at workplace, stalking, throwing of acid (on women), trafficking (of the girl child and women), and so on. There was a voluble demand for introduction of death penalty for rapists. In view of the development, a Commission of Enquiry headed by a former Chief Justice of India, Justice JS Verma, was appointed to deliberate on and suggest required changes in the related laws. The Commission duly made a number of recommendations.

As an immediate step for assuaging the public outrage, the President of India promulgated an Ordinance early in February 2013 amending drastically some of the existing provisions of law regarding rape and other forms of gender violence. Later, the government, following further deliberations by a Group of Ministers (GoM) and keeping in view the vibrant public sentiment, came up with a comprehensive Bill, now famously known as 'The CRIMINAL

LAW (AMENDMENT) ACT 2013 (Act No. 63-C of 2013). The Act duly passed by Parliament in March 2013 introduces a number of fundamental amendments into the IPC, the Cr.P.C. 1973, the Indian Evidence Act 1872 and the Protection of Children from Sexual Offences Act 2012. It can be said to be a landmark in the history of women's empowerment in India since proper implementation of its provisions will go a long way to enhance security of women from the onslaught of gender-based offenders.

Following are the main new features of the Act codifying for the first time in the statute book certain 'offences against women' that will be liable for stringent penal action:

1. Failure of the police to register an FIR (Section 166A IPC);
2. Non-treatment of the victim at hospital (Section 166B IPC);
3. Causing of hurt by acid or attempt to do so (Sections 326A and 326B IPC)
4. Sexual harassment as defined broadly by the Supreme Court in 'Vishaka vs the State of Rajasthan' (Section 354A IPC);
5. Use of criminal force on a woman with intent to disrobe her (Section 354B IPC);
6. Voyeurism (Section 354C IPC);
7. Stalking (Section 354D IPC);
8. Trafficking of women and minors (section 370 IPC);
9. Exploitation of trafficked women and children (Section 370A);
10. New definition of the offence of Rape – that, among other things, includes fellatio and cunnilingus (Section 375 IPC as amended).
11. Age of consent has been raised to 18 years. This means that consent of the woman for sex is immaterial if her age is below 18 years. It will be treated as rape even if she had consented for the same.
12. The minimum punishment for a rape offender shall be 7 years and could extend to life imprisonment. It could be death penalty for repeat offenders (Section 376E IPC).

13. A rape offender inflicting on a woman such injuries that result in the death or a persistent vegetative state of the victim (remember the case of Aruna Shaubag) will receive a sentence of imprisonment for the remainder of his natural life, or, in appropriate cases, a sentence of death (Section 376A IPC). The period of punishment cannot be less than 20 years in any case. Similar punishment will be there for gang rape also (Section 376D IPC);
14. Punishment for eve-teasing has been enhanced to imprisonment for 3 years (Section 509 IPC as amended);
15. A women police officer shall record the 'first information' given by a rape victim. Otherwise, such information may be recorded by a police officer at the victim's residence in presence of an interpreter or educator. The recording of such information by an officer shall be video-graphed. The investigating police officer shall, as soon as possible, get the statement of the victim recorded by a judicial magistrate. (Section 154 Cr PC. as amended).
16. Statement of a victim of gender violence is to be recorded by a woman police officer, or alternatively, any woman officer of the government (Section 161 Cr. P.C. as amended). This relates to the IO's case diary.
17. Sanction for prosecution will not be necessary when a public servant is accused of the above offences against women (Section 197 Cr.PC – Explanation).
18. The trial court shall ensure that a victim below 18 years of age does not have to 'confront' the offender in the court (Section 273 Cr.PC).
19. The trial of the above cases shall be conducted on a day to day basis and in any case shall be concluded within a period of two months from the date of the filing of the charge-sheet by the police (Section 309 Cr.PC).
20. The compensation payable by the State Government under Section 357A Cr.P.C. shall be in addition to the payment to the victim of the amount of fine imposed on the offender under Section 326A or 376D of the IPC.

21. All hospitals, public or private, whether run by the central or the state government, local bodies or any other person, shall provide first aid or medical treatment free of cost to the victims of the above offences.

22. In case of rape-related offences, it will not be permissible for the defence to raise a question on the victim's moral character or previous sexual experience (Section 146 Evidence Act).

Index

Other Valuable Books of Related Interest

Conspiracy to Kill Rajiv Gandhi: From CBI Files, by K Ragothaman (Former SP - CBI)

India's Spy Agencies: Shaken not Stirred, by Sunil S Parihar

Amazing Ladakh: Travel, trckking, religion, culture, wildlife almost everything about Leh-Kargil-Zanskar-Siachen, by Parvez Dewan, IAS

Heroes of North East India, by Sumitra Mukherjee

The 21st Century Army: Strategies for Future, by Lt Gen Gautam Banerjee, PVSM, AVSM, YSM

Jungle Warfare: An Ultimate Handbook by Dr NC Asthana, IPS

Ultimate Handbook of Urban Warfare by Dr NC Asthana, IPS

Army Leadership, by Department of Army, US

Counter Insurgency Guide, by Bureau of Political-Military Affairs, US

Lens and the Guerrilla: Insurgency in India's Northeast, by Rajeev Bhattacharya **(fully Illustrated)**

Intelligence Tradecraft: Secrets of Spy Warfare, by MK Dhar (former Joint Director, IB)

Manas Police & Security Yearbook 2010-2011 (fully Illustrated) by Ajit Doval IPS, BR Lall, IPS and other Top Cops.

Manas Defence Year Book 2010-2011 (Fully Illustrated) by General S Padmanabhan and Lt Gen S Pattabhiraman

CBI Top-Cop Recalls by SK Dutta, IPS (Former Director – CBI)

Pakistan's Intelligence by Sudhakar Raje (Ex-Indian Diplomat)

Who Runs Police? Secrets of a Top Cop by HS Swan, IPS (Ex-DGP, Haryana)

Is It Police? Confessions of a Top Cop by Vinay Kumar Singh, IPS

Police and Naxalism: Strategies for Solutions by ML Kumawat, IPS, Nazrul Islam, IPS and others

Common Man's Guide to Police & Criminal Laws by Dr DV Guruprasad, IPS (DG – Karnataka Police)

Rainbow People: Reinventing Northeast India by Falguni Rajkumar, IAS (Former Sec NEC)

Industrial Security: Management & Strategies by DC Nath, IPS & Capt SB Tyagi

Intelligence, Security & Asymmetric Warfare by Dhirendra Singh, IAS and Lt Gen DB Shekatkar

Intelligence for Management by DC Pathak, IPS (Former Dir-Intelligence Bureau)

Inside IB and RAW: The Rolling Stone that Gathered Moss by K Sankaran Nair, IPS (Former Head: Research and Analysis Wing (RAW)

Intelligence: Corporate Success and Vigilance by D C Pathak, IPS (Ex Chief – IB)

The Undisclosed Punjab: India Besieged by Terror by Birbal Nath, IPS (Former DGP, Punjab)

The Folds of Insurgency by AP Maheshwari, IPS

Who Owns CBI? The Naked Truth by BR Lall, IPS (Former: Joint Director, CBI)

Saga of Civil Services by Dr Yogendra Narain, IAS (Former Defence Secretary)

Open Secrets: India's Intelligence Unveiled by M K Dhar, IPS

Security Manual by P Benjamin

SPYMASTER: My Life in the CIA by Ted Shackley

VIP Security: What You Need to know by Kanchan Sinha

Armed Forces Tribunal by Dr UC Jha

Beyond North East: Insurgency-History-Development by HN Das (Former Chief Secretary, Assam)

Why Bureaucracy Fails by Kalyan Ray, IAS

WMD Terrorism: Strategy for Consequences Management by Brig MS Patial

Intelligence Manual by Department of Defence, USA

The ISI Game Plan by Brig Yash Mohan, VSM

Terror, Insurgency and the State: Ending Protracted Conflicts by Marianne Heiberg etc.

Operation Triple X: An Indian Spy-Run in Pakistan A Novel by MK Dhar, IPS

Naxalism: Causes and Cure by PK Agrawal, IAS

Legal Safeguards for Defence Personnel by Air Cmde. Ranvir Kumar (Former Judge Advocate General)

Reforming Intelligence Agencies: Pakistan's Transitional Democracy by Frederic Grare

Combating Terrorism: Strategies of Ten Countries by Yonah Alexander

Strategies in Defence and Intelligence by Lt Gen S Pattabhiraman & MK Dhar, IPS

Sports, Games and Adventure Sports by Air Cmde (Dr) CN Ghosh

The Craft of Intelligence by Allen W Dulles

Fulcrum of Evil: ISI-CIA-Al Qaeda Nexus by MK Dhar (Former Joint Chief of IB)

The Conspirators: Fiction of Facts (A Book on Pakistan's Intelligence) by Brig Yash Mohan, VSM

Silent Warfare: Understanding the World of Intelligence by Abram N Shulsky & Gary J Schmitt

Wages of Crime: Black Markets, Illegal Finance and the Underworld Economy by R T Naylor

The Peace Keepers: Indian Police Service (IPS) by SR Arun, IPS

Para-Military Forces: Central Reserve and Foreign Policy by Dr AK Pasha

Human Rights Training by Dr S Subramanian, IPS

Industrial Espionage: Causes and Cure by Dr S Subramaniam, IPS

Executive Protection by Dr S Subramaniam, IPS

CIA's Eye on South Asia by Anuj Dhar, Journalist

Threat to Security: How Secured is India from within by PC Dogra, IPS (Former DGP, Punjab)

Effective Interrogation: Naxalism, Police, Intelligence by G Chatterjee (Former Intelligence Officer)

Financial Terrorism: Black Money and the Indian Elite by BR Lall, IPS (Former: Joint Director, CBI)

White Collar Crimes X-Posed by Thakur Shailendra Nath

Some of our learned Authors

General S Padmanabhan; General VP Malik; Air Chief Marshal Fali Homi Major; Admiral Vishnu Bhagwat; Admiral Nirmal Verma; Admiral Arun Prakash; Vice Admiral Vijay Shankar; Lt Gen Arjun Ray; Dr A Sivathanu Pillai DRDO; Parvez Dewan IAS; Dhirendra Singh IAS; Kalyan Ray IAS; Sangeeta Goel IAS; HN Das IAS; Dr Surender Ghonkrokta IAS; Falguni Rajkumar IAS; G Sundaram IAS; PS Bhatnagar IAS; N Vittal IAS; PK Agrawal IAS; Sudhir S Baloeria IAS; NS Sisodia IAS; Dhirendra Singh IAS; Dr Yogendra Narain IPS; JK Bagchi IAS; TSR Subramanian IAS; Prakash Singh IPS; DC Nath IPS; Ajit Doval IPS; SP Mathur IPS; MK Dhar IPS; SK Datta IPS; HS Swan IPS; BR Lall IPS; PC Dogra IPS; DC Pathak IPS; ML Kumawat IPS; Dr. S Subramanian IPS; RK Ohri IPS; RB Sreekumar IPS; Kalyan K Mitra IPS; RS Gupta IPS; K Koshy IPS; Kuldeep Khoda IPS; Ajay Kashyap IPS; Dr N Dilip Kumar IPS; Dr Nazrul Islam IPS; Dr DV Guruprasad IPS; AP Maheshwari IPS; Loknath Behera IPS; Dr NC Asthana IPS; PM Nair IPS; Dr Sundari Nanda IPS; Keshav Kumar IPS; Dr Prateep V Philip IPS; Muktesh Chander IPS; Dr PS Pasricha IPS; VK Agarwal IRS; Virendra Gupta IFS; Lt Gen SK Sinha; Lt Gen Raj Kadyan; Lt Gen Mukesh Sabharwal; Lt Gen HB Kala; Lt Gen PC Katoch; Lt Gen Gautam Banerjee; Lt Gen Ashok Kapur; Vice Admiral Suresh Bangara; Lt Gen CK Kapur; Lt Gen NS Narahari; Lt Gen Chandra Shekhar; Lt Gen ML Chibber; Lt Gen Ashok Joshi; Lt Gen DB Shekatkar; Lt Gen SRR Aiyengar; Lt Gen Utpal Bhattacharyya; Lt Gen Kamal Davar; Lt Gen Amitav Mukherji; Maj Gen Nilendra Kumar; Maj Gen Vinod Saighal; Maj Gen VK Singh; Maj Gen Anjan Mukherjee; Maj Gen Raj Mehta; Maj Gen Samay Ram; Maj Gen Y Behl; Maj Gen GD Bakshi; Gen Deepak Kapoor; Air Marshal SR Deshpande; Air Marshal RC Bajpai; Air Chief Marshal PV Naik; Air Vice Marshal AK Tiwary; Air Cmde (Dr) CN Ghosh; Ambassador Kishan S Rana IFS; Cmde Ranjit B Rai; Capt (IN) Alok Bansal; VK Singal IRS; Sudha Raman; Brig Yash Mohan; Brig Trigunesh Mukherjee; Brig. MS Patial; Col PK Gautam; Col Arun Jha; Col MS Jaswal; Col Anil Shorey; Lt Col Anil Bhatt; Dr Harsh Vardhan; Ratan Sharda, Sudhakar Raje; Dr RK Tiwari; Anuj Dhar, Journalist; Ranjit Kumar, Journalist; SK Vikram; Gopal Chowdhuri; Dr Pramod Sharma; Swati Sharma, etc.